THE UNOFFICIAL BOOK OF
CRICUT
CRAFTS

Also by Crystal Allen

Caticorn Crafts

THE UNOFFICIAL BOOK OF
CRICUT
CRAFTS

The Ultimate Guide to
Your Electric Cutting Machine

CRYSTAL ALLEN

Skyhorse Publishing

Skyhorse Publishing books may be purchased in bulk at special discounts for sales promotion, corporate gifts, fund-raising, or educational purposes. Special editions can also be created to specifications. For details, contact the Special Sales Department, Skyhorse Publishing, 307 West 36th Street, 11th Floor, New York, NY 10018 or info@skyhorsepublishing.com.

Skyhorse® and Skyhorse Publishing® are registered trademarks of Skyhorse Publishing, Inc.®, a Delaware corporation.

Visit our website at www.skyhorsepublishing.com.

10 9 8 7 6

Library of Congress Cataloging-in-Publication Data is available on file.

Cover design by Daniel Brount
Cover photo credit: Crystal Allen

Print ISBN: 978-1-5107-5714-1
Ebook ISBN: 978-1-5107-5715-8

Printed in China

To my sisters—

The sister I was born with.

The sister I gained through marriage.

The sisters who started as friends and then became family.

And to all my sisters in the crafting world, because through our creativity we are all connected!

CONTENTS

INTRODUCTION

Hi, crafty friends! I'm so excited you have discovered this book and that we get to craft together! I'm Crystal Allen, and I'm the owner of Hello Creative Family. If you are reading this book, then chances are you fall into one of four categories:

1. You've heard about the amazing things that Cricut cutting machines can do, and you're considering buying one. (Do it!!! Your life will be forever changed.)
2. You've recently purchased a Cricut, it's still sitting in its box, you're feeling overwhelmed, and you're looking for a bit of help. (You've come to the right place! I can't wait to help you get that bad boy out of the box and set up so you can get crafting!)
3. You're a Cricut newbie, you've unboxed your Cricut, you've cut your first few projects, but now you're feeling overwhelmed by ALL THE THINGS it can do. (We're going to have so much fun. Before you know it, you're going to be a Cricut expert and will be cutting this, that, and everything with your Cricut.)
4. You're a Cricut expert, your Cricut is your "ride or die" craft tool, you know it can do so many amazing things, and you're here for some extra crafty inspiration! (Yay!!! I hope you're inspired by the 40 projects in this book and that you have so much fun with it.)

I'm so happy to be writing this book, because I've been in all four of the categories listed above! I was pretty new to the craft blogging world the first time I heard about the Cricut. My crafty friends told me it was amazing, that I needed one, and that my crafting life would be forever changed once I owned a Cricut Explore. A month later, I was at a blogging conference where Cricut was a sponsor for an evening party. They had a table set up in each corner of the room where they were showing people how to use their amazing cutting machines. All around me, people were eating, dancing, and having a grand celebration, but I only had eyes for those incredible cutting machines. The table in the far corner of the room was completely abandoned, so I went over, sat myself down next to a Cricut employee, and spent the next three hours asking her every question I could possibly think of and learning about this incredible machine.

A month later, my first Cricut was delivered and my crafting life has been forever changed—truly. It's been six years since the first time I used a Cricut, and this incredible machine has taken my crafting abilities to a whole new level. My Cricut is by far my favorite craft tool—and I know you'll love yours too!

I've broken this book into four sections:

Which Cricut Is Right For You?

In this section, I will share the differences between the Cricut Explore Air 2, the Cricut Maker, and the new (as of time of press) Cricut Joy, review which materials each machine cuts, and help you determine which machine is right for you!

Unboxing Your Cricut and Setting Up

I can't tell you how many people have told me that they've bought a Cricut and it's been sitting in a box in their craft room for six months or longer! I'm going to show you how easy it is to unbox your Cricut, get it set up, and create your very first project.

Cricut Design Space 101

Design Space is amazing! Once you know how to use it, the sky is the limit for what you can create! I'm going to walk you through the basics and, before you know it, you'll be using Design Space like a pro!

40 Projects Using Cricut's Most Popular Materials

You have your Cricut, it's all set up, you know how to use Design Space—now it's time for the real fun to begin! We're breaking out the most popular materials to cut with your Cricut and giving you 40 projects you can make with your machine! Projects are divided into eight sections:

- Vinyl
- Paper
- HTV
- Fabric
- Basswood, Balsa wood, and Chipboard
- Leather
- Infusible Ink
- Specialty Materials

Each chapter starts with a breakdown about that material, tips and tricks for using it, lingo, and other supplies and tools that you may want to have on hand when cutting that material.

My main goal for this section of the book is to give you a wide variety of ways you can use each type of material. For example, in the section about HTV, I show you how to apply HTV to clothing, wood, paper napkins, home decor items, and canvas bags. My hope is that once you try each project, it will blow the door wide open to a whole world of incredible, creative ideas for things you can make with your Cricut!

Are you ready to get started?

Credit: Brooke Berry

My favorite thing to talk about is Cricut crafts, so I'd love to hear from you! Visit **hellocreativefamily.com**, send me a message, and show me what you've been making by using the hashtag #hcfcricutcrafts and tagging **@hellocreativefamily** on Instagram! I can't wait to Cricut with you!

WHICH CRICUT IS RIGHT FOR YOU?

Cricut Maker

You've seen all the amazing Cricut crafts your friends have made on Facebook. You've been dazzled by your favorite influencers' Cricut creations on Instagram. You've pinned more than a few *incredible* Cricut projects on Pinterest. And now you've made the decision—it's time to buy a Cricut! Yay! I am so excited for you! Now the only question is: Which one to buy? The Cricut Joy, the Cricut Explore Air 2, or the Cricut Maker?

The first thing to note is that the Cricut Maker can do everything that the Cricut Explore Air can, and more. If money isn't a consideration, then I highly suggest you buy the Cricut Maker.

Let's be honest, though—money is a consideration for most of us. So, what's the difference between the Cricut Maker and the Cricut Explore Air 2? Let's compare the two machines, shall we?

Cricut Explore Air 2

Cricut Joy

EXPLORE VERSUS MAKER

CRICUT CAPABILITIES	EXPLORE	MAKER
Simple to learn to use	✓	✓
Cuts, writes, and scores 100 materials	✓	✓
Cuts, writes, and scores over 300 materials		✓
Bluetooth capable	✓	✓
Two tool holders	✓	✓
Setting for 2 times faster cutting and writing	✓	✓
10 times more cutting pressure		✓
Compatible with Cricut's Adaptive Tool Set		✓
Rotary Blade for cutting fabric		✓
Knife Blade for cutting thicker materials including chipboard and basswood		✓
Scoring Wheels for creating creases perfect for paper crafts		✓
Engraving Tip for creating engraved handmade items		✓
Debossing Tip for creating debossed designs		✓
Wavy Blade for creating wavy edges quickly and seamlessly		✓
Perforation blade for creating evenly spaced perforated tear-offs		✓

What about the Cricut Joy?

The Cricut Joy was announced and released to the crafting world after this book was written, so I haven't had the chance to get to use it to the same level as the Cricut Maker or Cricut Explore Air. We definitely didn't want to release the book without giving you some information about the Cricut Joy, though, so here's what I know about it after my limited time spent using it.

The Cricut Joy is Cricut's new mini-but-mighty cutting machine. Weighing in at less than four pounds, the Cricut Joy makes crafting anywhere and everywhere easy! The new technology in this machine lets you cut Cricut brand Smart Vinyl, Smart Iron-on, and Smart Infusible Ink without a mat!

One of the biggest features (besides the portability) that has given this tiny cutting machine such a big buzz is the matless technology. When using Cricut's "Smart" product, you can cut a single design that is 4.5 inches in width by 4 feet in length, repeated up to 20 feet in length.

Another feature that has paper crafters especially excited is the Cricut Joy Card Mat. The mat has a folder on top that allows you to insert the back half of a pre-made blank Cricut Card into the folder, keeping it protected so that you cut only the top part of the card.

The Cricut Joy can cut 50 materials including iron-on, vinyl, Infusible Ink Transfer Sheets, cardstock, and Smart Labels. You can find the full list in the Appendix: Which Materials Can Each Cricut Cut section of this book (page 281).

The Cricut Joy is an incredible little machine that makes crafting portable and is perfect for small spaces. The capabilities aren't as wide as with the Cricut Maker and Cricut Explore Air 2, however, this machine is a fabulous starter machine and perfect for crafters with small spaces, people who want to craft on the go, kids and classrooms, or for people who don't see themselves creating projects that are more than 4.5 inches in width.

What is the Cricut Maker Adaptive Tool System?

The biggest difference between the Cricut Maker and the Cricut Explore Air 2 is the invention of the Adaptive Tool System, which the Cricut Maker has and the Cricut Joy and Cricut Explore Air 2 do not. Unique to the Cricut Maker, the Adaptive Tool system brings together three major technologies that give professional class–cutting versatility and performance:

1. Delivers 10 times (almost 9 pounds/4 kilograms) more cutting force than the Explore line! Now that's a lot of power!
2. Uses a sophisticated steering system to actively control the direction of the blade at all times. (That's what the shiny gold teeth at the top of each tool do!)

3. Tests to be sure you are using the correct blade before it starts cutting and tells you to change it if necessary . . . which makes this system pretty much goof-proof!

Knife Blade   Rotary Blade   Scoring Wheels

Basic   Fine   Wavy   Engraving
Perforation Blade   Debossing Tip   Blade   Tip

At the time of writing this book, Cricut had eight Adaptive Tools available. Each of the tools that have a number (Scoring Wheels, Perforation Blade, Debossing Tip, Wavy Blade, and Engraving Tip) are part of the Maker's QuickSwap Toolset, which means you only need one housing and can change the tool tip with a push of a button. To change the tool tips, you simply press the button at the top of the housing, which releases the tip and allows you to put on a new one!

Cricut Knife Blade:

Every DIYers dream! Use the knife blade to cut through thicker materials such as balsa wood, basswood, chipboard, tooling leather, garment leather, craft foam, and matboard! The knife blade makes multiple, precise cuts with the Maker's increased cutting force to deliver amazing results.

Cricut Rotary Blade:

This handy tool is every sewer's dream! Say bye-bye to your handheld rotary cutter and let your Cricut Maker do all the precision cutting for you! The rotary blade can cut beautiful designs through a variety of fabrics and materials, including felt, quilter's cotton, denim, canvas, silk, and crepe paper! It lets you spend time doing what every seamstress loves—sewing!

Cricut Scoring Wheel and Double Scoring Wheel #1&2:

Make beautiful cards, tags, gift boxes, 3D home décor, and more with Cricut's two professional-quality scoring wheels. These single and double scoring wheels can score thin, thick, and coated paper using ten times more pressure than Cricut's Scoring Stylus, giving you sharp creases that fold with ease.

Cricut Basic Perforation Blade #11:

Create a neat tear line every time with Cricut's Perforation blade! Use the perforation blade to create coupon books, raffle tickets, peel-aways, and more! The perforation blade creates evenly spaced perforations for both straight and curved lines as well as shapes. Works with different types of paper, poster board, acetate, and more!

Cricut Fine Debossing Tip #21:

The dream tool for every paper crafter! Get rid of those debossing folders and create your own highly detailed, personalized debossed designs using the Cricut Debossing Tip! Use for cards, gift tags, gift boxes, planner dashboards, and more! Works beautifully on leather, cardstock, coated paper, basswood, and other materials.

Cricut Wavy Blade #31:

Create a fun, wavy line out of paper, fabric, iron-on, and vinyl using the Cricut Wavy Blade! The wavy blade takes much less time to cut than a regular blade because of its specially sculpted stainless steel blade. Create fun finished edges on envelopes, cards, vinyl decals, and more!

Cricut Engraving Tip #41:

The Cricut Engraving Tip is every jewelry maker's dream come true! Engrave on a wide variety of metal jewelry blanks to create pet tags, bracelets, necklaces, art pieces, and other personalized keepsakes! The engraving tip can be used to engrave text, monograms, decorative flourishes, and other fun designs to create one-of-a-kind handmade items.

Let's break it down:

- Because the Cricut Maker uses an Adaptive Tool System, it's able to cut more than 300 different types of material, and there are new ones being added consistently as Cricut releases new Adaptive Tools.
- The Cricut Explore Air 2 can cut more than 100 different types of material, which is still amazing, and has a lower price point than the Cricut Maker.
- The Cricut Maker can do all the things that the Cricut Explore Air 2 can do (and then some), so if money isn't a consideration or you are a hardcore crafter, then the Cricut Maker is definitely the machine for you.
- If you're on a budget and/or are just getting started with crafting, then the Cricut Explore Air 2 might be a fabulous option for you—and you can always upgrade later!

I would suggest thinking about all the things you would love to make with your Cricut and taking a look at the cutting material lists in this book (page 281) to determine which machine is right for you.

Additionally, as you flip through the pages of this book, check to see which projects you would most like to try, and see which machine can be used for those projects. Many of them can be made with either the Cricut Maker or Cricut Explore Air 2, but there are some that can only be made with the Cricut Maker. For a quick visual check, I used my pink Cricut for all projects that you can make using a Cricut Explore or a Cricut Maker and my white-and-gold Cricut Maker for all projects that can only be made with a Maker.

For me, the big selling points for the Cricut Maker were the rotary cutter tool for cutting fabric; the knife blade for cutting chipboard, basswood, and balsa wood; and the engraving tip for engraving on metal. Those four materials make the investment into a Cricut Maker worth the extra money in my eyes.

Unboxing Your Cricut and Setting Up

So, you've picked the Cricut that's right for you. You've gone to the craft store to pick it up or have waited patiently for it to arrive in the mail. It's the big day! Time to unbox your brand new Cricut! Are you excited? I feel like Cricut owners fall into one of two categories:

1. The people who dive right in and unbox their Cricut as soon as humanly possible.
2. The people who leave their Cricut in the box for months, who want more than anything to start crafting but are feeling daunted.

No matter which category you fall into, I've got your back! Unboxing your Cricut and setting it up for the first time is so simple! I'm going to walk you through each step of unboxing so you'll be all set to get your Cricut out and start having fun with it!

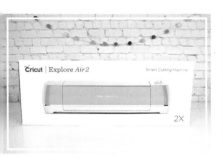 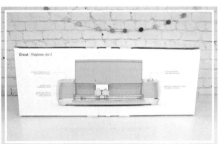 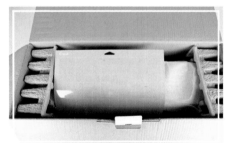

When purchasing your Cricut Maker or Cricut Explore Air 2 from the Cricut website, you'll have the option of buying just the machine or a machine bundle. Most craft stores sell just the machine (not bundles). Regardless of whether you get a machine or a machine bundle, your Cricut is going to come in a box, and each box will come with the same basic components inside. They are:

- Your Cricut Cutting Machine
- Cutting mat
- Power cord
- USB cord for connecting your Cricut to your computer
- A pen
- Cutting blade (This may be loaded inside of your Cricut, so don't panic if you don't see it right away.)
- Let's Get Started packet (This will have an instruction book, step-by-step guide for setting up your new machine, materials for a new project, and a trial membership for Cricut Access.)

Let's Get Started Unboxing Your Machine!

Step 1: Remove everything from the box and make sure that all the components are there for your machine. Check the side of the box for the list of the pieces that come with your machine.

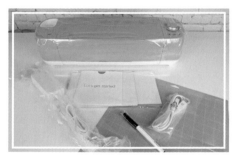

Step 2: Remove the plastic covering from your Cricut.

Step 3: Open the "Let's Get Started" packet.

Step 4: Turn your Cricut around and plug in the power cord.

Step 5: Go to cricut.com/setup and follow the instructions to connect your Cricut via Windows, Mac, IOS, or Android.

Note: If you already have a Cricut, navigating to cricut.com/setup will take you straight to Design Space. Connect your Cricut to your computer with the USB cord, click on a project you want to make, click "Make It," and Design Space will connect to your new machine.

To learn how to connect your Cricut's bluetooth connection with Windows, Mac, IOS or Android, go to https://tinyurl.com/cricutbluetooth.

Step 6: Now you're ready to make! Your Cricut will come with a project that's perfect for a first timer! We'd love to suggest that you make a bit of bling for your Cricut as one of your first projects! It's simple. Visit our #Creative Cricut Bling project on page 51 of the book. It's a simple project for first timers and lets you make something that you'll see every time you use your Cricut so that you'll always remember your first project!

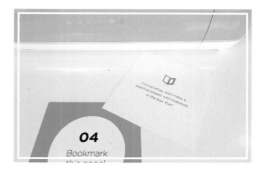

CRICUT DESIGN SPACE 101

Ready to start using your Cricut? Whether your design idea is extremely simple, or intricate and complex, you can't cut a project using your Cricut cutting machine without using Cricut Design Space!

If you're a technophobe like me, the thought of mastering a new computer program can seem overwhelming. You're in luck for two reasons:

1. You've got me here to walk you through it!
2. Cricut's design software is extremely easy to use if you know the basics, and you can build on more advanced techniques the more you use it.

Cricut will automatically prompt you to download Design Space during your machine setup. Once you have it downloaded, click on the Cricut C application icon to open the program, and let's get started!

In this chapter of the book, I'm going to walk you through using Cricut Design Space on your computer. Cricut Design Space is also available as an app for iOS and Android users. The abilities between the desktop version and the app version of Design Space are all very similar, so you may just have to poke around to figure out where each tool lives.

First Glance

When you open Cricut Design Space, you'll be brought to a home screen with lots of options for things you can do.

Along the top of the screen, you'll see clickable photos of featured machines and supplies you can buy from Cricut.com. You'll probably also see an advertisement for Cricut Access; more on that later.

Below the advertisements, you'll see a category called My Projects, with a box that has a + sign within a circle that says New Project.

Below that, you'll see different categories of ready-to-make projects. These are projects created by Cricut, Cricut brand partners, and Cricut Community Members that have already been designed and can be cut with the push of a button.

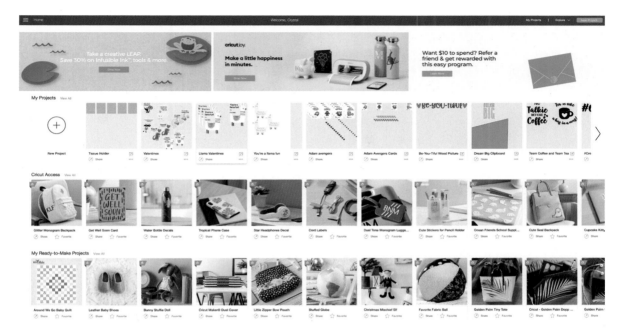

This is your Home screen. Top line shows Cricut promotions. Second line shows "New Project" button and projects you've created and saved. Third and fourth lines show ready-to-make projects. Notice the green A in corner of some photos, which means you can make them for free with a Cricut Access subscription.

On some of the photos, you will see a green A. The green A is a symbol for Cricut Access and lets you know that if you have a Cricut Access membership, this cut file is free for you to use.

What is Cricut Access?

Cricut Access is a subscription service that Cricut sells that gives you instant, free access to 100,000+ images, 100+ fonts, and hundreds of ready-to-make projects. Cricut Access members also receive a discount on Cricut purchases including ordering supplies from Cricut.com and licensed images through Design Space.

Cricut Access memberships are available billed monthly or annually.

When you purchase a Cricut cutting machine, it comes with a free month subscription to Cricut Access, which gives you a good opportunity to try out the service.

If you're not a Cricut Access member, you can still access images, fonts, and ready-to-make projects, but you'll have to pay a small, one-time fee to use them.

Creating a Blank Canvas

When you click on the New Project button, you'll be brought to a blank Cricut canvas.

At the top left side of the screen, you'll see three lines stacked on top of each other. When you click here, it will bring up a menu.

Main Menu

Home
Canvas
New Machine Setup
Calibration
Manage Custom Materials
Update Firmware
Account Details
Link Cartridges

Cricut Access
Settings
Legal
New Features
The Country You Live In
Help
Sign Out
Feedback

If you ever navigate away from your canvas and can't figure out how to get back, simply click on this menu and select **Canvas** to return to the canvas you were working on.

The other categories you should know under this menu include:

Calibration: Use this function to calibrate your machine's blade for more accurate cuts when using the Print and Cut function as well as the Cricut Maker Knife Blade.

Link Cartridge: Your average Cricut user will never need to use this menu option; however, if you're the lucky owner of any old Cricut cartridges, you'll want to know this one! Click this button, enter your cartridge details, and you're now able to use the images from the cartridge within Cricut Design Space.

Settings: Under this menu item, you can choose whether your canvas has a full grid, partial grid, or no grid. You can also select if your measurements are shown in metric or imperial and where you would like your work saved for offline use.

Design Space settings

Canvas grid
● Full Grid   ○ Partial Grid   ○ No Grid

Units
● Imperial   ○ Metric

Saving for Offline
● Cloud & Computer   ○ Cloud Only

Exploring Your Toolbars

Left-Side Toolbar

The left-side toolbar is where all the big stuff happens. It's broken down into seven buttons.

New: Click this button whenever you would like to create a new canvas. Cricut only lets you work on one canvas at a time, so make sure you save your current canvas before creating a new one.

Templates: Sometimes you have a project idea that seems great in your head, but you just don't know how it will look once implemented. Enter Cricut templates!

Cricut has created drawings of some of the most popular "blanks" for Cricuting on. Pick a blank, lay your design over the top, and get a sneak peek of what the finished product will look like.

Examples of some of the many templates Cricut a Design Space has to choose from.

An example of Cricut's bib blank with the Homegrown SVG from page 223 of this book laid on top.

Pro-Crafter Tip

Measure the item you're cricuting on with a tape measure and then use the custom-size option to size your template on screen to the same dimensions. This will give you a much more accurate view of what your finished project will look like.

Projects: This button brings up a variety of ready-to-make projects. Use the Category and Search boxes in the upper right-hand toolbar to narrow down the type of projects you're looking for.

Images: This section is where you find every single image available in Cricut Designs Space, including images available to purchase, images included with Cricut Access, and images you have uploaded.

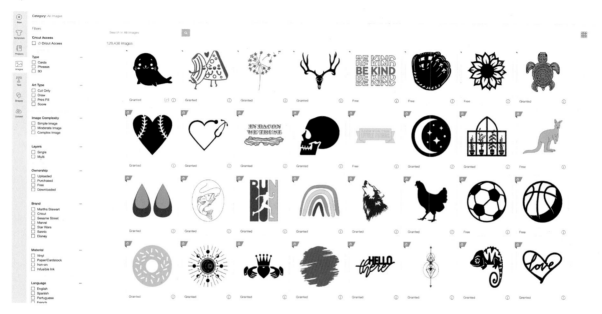

Filter categories include:

Cricut Access (images included for free with a subscription)
Type
Art Type
Image Complexity

Layers
Ownership
Material
Language

Pro-Crafter Tip

Each image available through Design Space is part of an image set. I have often found that if I like one image, there are other images in the set that I also like. To find what image sets an image you like is part of, click on the "i" in the lower right-hand corner of the image.

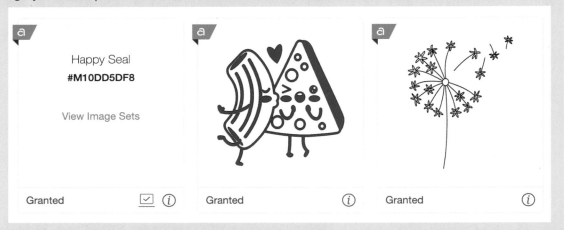

You will then see the title of the image, the image number, and a green clickable line that says "View Image Sets." Click this line to see all images included in this set.

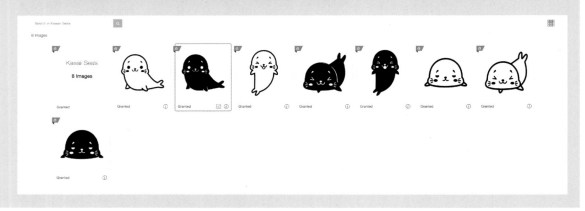

Text: When you want to add words to your canvas, clicking Text is the place to start! You'll want to fine-tune your text with a bit of help from your top toolbar. Read all about that in the text toolbar section!

Shapes: Cricut provides its users with 10 basic shapes that are 100 percent free to use. They include a square, circle, triangle, diamond, pentagon, hexagon, star, octagon, heart, and score line. You can access these basic shapes under the Shapes menu. If you're looking for these shapes with a bit more style or pizzazz, you can also find additional hearts, stars, squares, etc. under the Shapes menu included in Cricut Access or available for a one-time fee.

Upload: In my opinion, the Upload button is one of the most important buttons in all of Design Space. If you ever want to cut your own artwork or cut files that you find outside of Design Space, you'll need to know how to use this function. I refer to the upload button for almost every project in this book. It's so important that I think it deserves its own section in this book. So let's give it one, shall we?

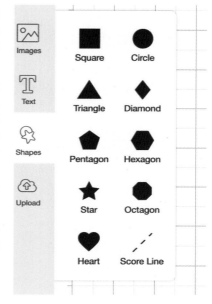

Shapes menu.

How to Upload Cut Files into Design Space

There are six kinds of images you can upload to Design Space: JPG, GIF, PNG, BMP, SVG, and DXF files. You can also upload patterns and photos to use to fill layers, which is used for Cricut's Print and Cut function. I'm going to walk you through the basics of uploading the four most common types of design files to Design Space, which will give you the skills necessary to upload any cut file to Design Space.

Uploading an SVG to Design Space:

Click on **Upload** in the left-hand toolbar.
Click **Upload Image**, then select your cut file from your computer.

With an SVG file, the designer has already done all the work of creating different layers and telling the design file where to cut. All you need to do now is name your design and save it! Cricut also allows you to create tags for your design so that you can find it easily in the future.

After you save your image, you'll be taken to a screen where you see all of the images that you have uploaded. Click the image you would like to use and then click **Insert Image**.

Uploading a PNG to Design Space:

Click on **Upload** in the left-hand toolbar.

Click **Upload Image**, then select your cut file from your computer.

Choose whether your design is simple, moderately complex, or complex. For most designs, I find that simple works fine. Click **Continue**.

Continued >>

If your PNG has a transparent background, then the work will all be done for selecting the areas that you want cut. (If your PNG doesn't have a transparent background then follow the instructions for how to upload a JPG to Design Space.)

Click **Continue** and then save your image as a cut file.

After you save your image, you'll be taken to a screen where you see all the images that you have uploaded. Click the image you would like to use and then click **Insert Image**.

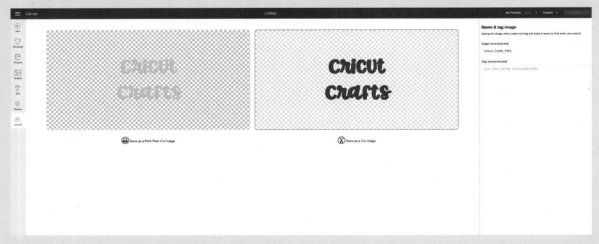

Uploading a JPG to Design Space:

Click on **Upload** in the left-hand toolbar.
Click **Upload Image**, then select your cut file from your computer.

Choose whether your design is simple, moderately complex, or complex. For most designs, I find that simple works fine. Click **Continue**.

Continued >>

Click on the areas of the image that you want to remove. Since the background isn't transparent, you will need to tell the Cricut where to cut.

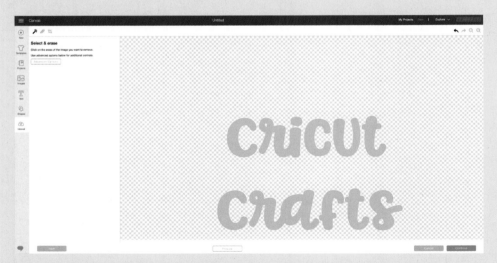

In this case, you click once in the white area outside of the letters and blue check boxes will appear all around the outside of the words. Next, click the inside letters like the center of the a, and the loops of the r's and s.

Click the **Preview** button to see what your cut file will look like and to make sure you haven't missed any areas. Click **Hide Preview** to go back to the regular view.

Click **Continue** and then save your image as a cut file.

After you save your image, you'll be taken to a screen where you can see all the images that you have uploaded. Click the image you would like to use and then click **Insert Image**.

Uploading a Print and Cut Image to Design Space:

Click on **Upload** in the left-hand toolbar.

Click **Upload Image**, then select your cut file from your computer.

Choose **Complex** image.

If your image doesn't have a transparent background, you 'll want to click on the areas of the image that you want to remove, telling the Cricut where to cut.

In this case, you would click once to the side or above the coffee cup and again in the handle of the coffee cup. Blue checkboxes will appear around the cup where you want your Cricut to cut away.

Click **Continue** and then save your image as a Print and Cut file.

After you save your image, you'll be taken to a screen where you can see all of the images you have uploaded. Click the image you would like to use and then click **Insert Image**.

To use a Print and Cut image, you'll use your home printer to print your image on a printable material like cardstock or printable vinyl, and then load it into your Cricut to be cut.

Top Toolbar

If the left-side toolbar is where all the big stuff happens, the top and right toolbars are where all the fine-tuning magic happens!

↶ ↷ **Undo and Redo Arrows:** Use these buttons to undo and redo changes you've made to the images on your canvas.

 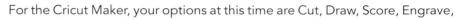 **Linetype:** Use this box to select what you want your Cricut to do with each of your shapes/images. When you're using the Cricut Explore, your options will be Cut, Draw, and Score.

For the Cricut Maker, your options at this time are Cut, Draw, Score, Engrave, Deboss, Wave, and Perf. As more Adaptive Tools are released, this list will grow.

For the Cricut Joy, your options will be Cut and Draw.

 Material Colors: To help keep which image will be cut from each color material straight, select different colors for each cut element from this box.

 Fill: This box is used when you will be printing elements using your home printer. "No Fill" means you will just be cutting that piece. "Print" means you will be printing then cutting.

Print Type Box: When you change your fill type to Print, you can select either colors or patterns from this box to fill your cut file with for the Print and Cut function.

Select/Deselect: Quickly select and deselect all the cut elements on your canvas using this button. Another way to select a cut element is to click and hold down your mouse on one corner of your screen and drag a box over all the elements you want to select. You can also click on each cut element you would like to select in the right-hand toolbar while holding down the Shift button on your keyboard to select.

Edit: Under the Edit box, you will find options for Cut, Copy, and Paste.

Align: To use the Align tool, you'll need to select two or more cut elements from your canvas. With this tool, you can align elements left, center horizontally, align right, align top, center vertically, align bottom, center, distribute horizontally, and distribute vertically. I use this tool frequently immediately before attaching, welding, or slicing pieces. More about those three tools in the next section.

Arrange: Design Space works in layers. The first element you add to your canvas will be on the bottom layer, and everything you add after will layer on top. Sometimes you will want an element to be sitting at a higher level than where it's at. Use the Arrange button to move elements all the way to the back, back one layer, forward one layer, or all the way to the front by using the Send to Back, Move Backward, Move Forward, and Send to Front options. This is another tool that I use frequently immediately before attaching, welding, or slicing pieces. More about those tools in the next section.

Flip: This tool allows you to flip your images horizontally and vertically.

Size: Resize your cut element using this block by changing the width and height boxes. The default is for your image to stay proportional; however, if you would like to change that, you can click the Lock button that sits over the "H" to unlock proportions.

You can also size an image by clicking on the image and using the arrow box that appears in the bottom right-hand corner of your image. To unlock the proportions when sizing this way, click the Lock that appears in the bottom left-hand corner of the image when it is selected.

Rotate: Use this button to rotate your image. I use this button frequently when adding score lines to a project.

Position: Move your image to exactly where you want it on your canvas by using the Position box. Positioning your image at 1X, 1Y will put your image 1 inch down and 1 inch over on your canvas. This number, however, does not correlate to where your image will be cut on your cutting mat. Positioning your image on the cutting mat can be done after you click Make It when you're editing your mat.

My Projects: Click on this button to be brought to a list of all of the projects that you have saved in Design Space. To return to your canvas from this screen, click Canvas on the left-hand side of the screen.

Save: Make sure you can revisit your project on another day by clicking the Save button. If you're only using elements from within Cricut Design Space, you will be allowed to save your file as public so that you can share the cut file with friends. If you're using any fonts or images that you have uploaded, you will only be allowed to save the file for personal use.

Machine Button: Pick the type of machine you're using (Cricut Maker, Cricut Explore, or Cricut Joy) from this dropdown menu to access features exclusive to that machine.

Make It: If you only know one button in Design Space, this is the button! Click Make It whenever you are ready to start cutting your project.

Text Toolbar

Once you have added text to your canvas, a text toolbar will appear below your top toolbar. (Note: You will only see it when your text is selected.) The tools included in this toolbar are:

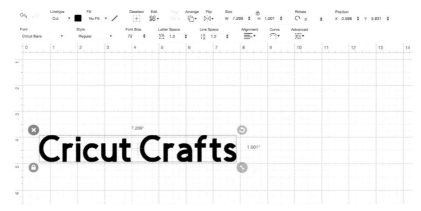

Font: When you press this button, it pulls up every font available for you to use, including Cricut fonts and fonts from your computer. You're able to sort fonts that you own versus fonts that are owned by Cricut by clicking the All, System, and Cricut buttons. There is also a box to search fonts by name as well as a filter box where you can filter fonts by categories that include My Fonts, Multi-Layer, Single Layer, Writing, and Saved For Offline.

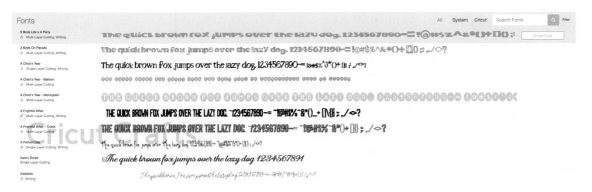

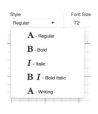

Style: Under the Style menu, you can make your font bold, italic, bold italic, writing, and back to regular again.

Font Size: Use the font size box to change the numerical value of the size of your font.

Letter Space: Use this function to move your letters closer together or further apart.

Line Spacing: Make the spaces between words stacked on top of each other closer together or farther apart.

Alignment: Change your font so that it is centered, left aligned, or right aligned.

Curve: This was one of Cricut's most requested features. Play with the slider under this box to quickly and easily give your words an arc.

Advanced: Under this menu, you're able to ungroup your words, making it easier to play with the spacing of both letters and lines. This tool is especially popular for people using script fonts to help connect letters. The three options available under this menu are Ungroup to Letters, Ungroup to Lines, and Ungroup to Layers.

Right-Side Toolbar

Last but not least, we have the right-side toolbar. Knowing how to properly use these tools will make designing in Design Space so much easier. The tools in this section include:

Group: Select two or more images in your project and press the Group button to group them together. Why would you want to do this? It's easier to move grouped images together on your canvas. Also, once you have the proportions figured out for your design, if your images are grouped together, when you resize one image it will automatically resize the other images it's grouped with, keeping it in the same proportions.

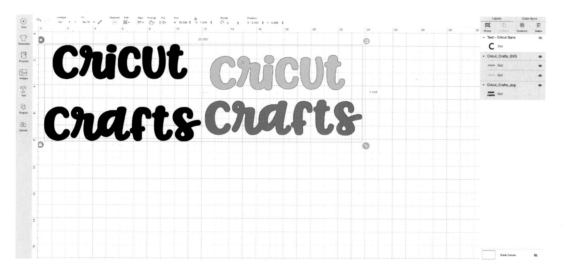

 Ungroup: Use this button to ungroup a set of images that have been grouped together.

 Duplicate: Duplicate whatever design element you have selected by pressing this button.

Delete: Delete whatever design element you have selected by pressing this button.

Slice: Slice and Weld are two of my very favorite functions within Design Space. Think of Slice like a cookie cutter. Lay one design element on top of another, select both pieces, select Slice, and Design Space will cut the top design out of the bottom design. For example, in this series of photos, I have laid the words *Cricut Crafts* on top of a heart. I then selected both pieces, pressed Slice, and I am left with the words *Cricut Crafts* cut out of the heart.

Weld: If Slice is like a cookie cutter, then Weld is like glue. Easily connect two or more design elements into one seamless piece by using the Weld button. For example, in this series of photos, I want to connect the heart to the end of the "s" in *cricut crafts*. I move the heart to the position where I want it, select both *cricut crafts* and the heart, and then click Weld. Design Space then turns the two pieces into one solid piece.

Attach: This button is used to group items of the same color so that they will cut the way you have them laid out on your cutting mat.

For example, let's say that I want these four hearts to cut so they're evenly spaced with 1 inch between each heart. If I space them on my canvas and don't attach them, then they will cut right next to each other to make the most effective use of your cutting material.

However, if I select all four hearts and attach them, they'll cut from the cutting mat the same way they're laid out on my canvas, making it easier to transfer to your project.

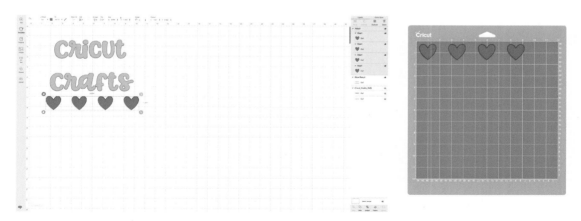

Detach: Once you have attached cut elements together, when you click on them, you'll see a Detach button appear where the Attach used to be. Press this button to detach your attached pieces.

Flatten: This button is used to turn elements into a Print and Cut image.

For example, in this series of photos, I have three different design elements: a white circle, aqua words that say *cricut crafts*, and four pink hearts. If I were to press Make It as it is, the design would cut from three different mats (one white, one aqua, and one pink).

However, if I select all three design elements and press Flatten, it will turn the design into one image that will print using your printer and then cut using your Cricut. The Cricut will cut around the outside of the circle and leave the rest intact.

Note: The largest size that the Cricut Print and Cut function will work with is 6.75 inches by 9.25 inches.

After You Click Make It

We've covered all the design tools in Design Space, but what happens after you click Make It? Let's walk through the basic steps for getting your project to cut.

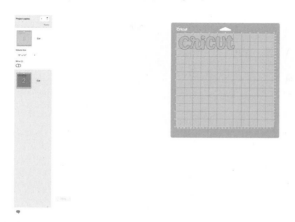

Once you click Make It, you will be taken to a screen that shows each of your cutting mats on the left-hand side of the screen. The first cutting mat will also be shown large on the screen.

Under each mat in the left-hand toolbar you will have two options:

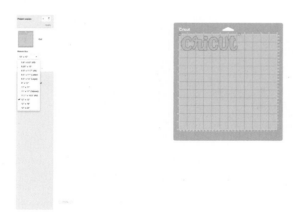

1. You can choose your material size from a dropdown list.

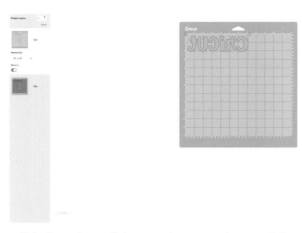

2. You can click the mirror slider to mirror your image. Mirroring is an important step to take when working with materials that cut with the correct side facing down on the mat like iron-on and Infusible Ink. If you don't mirror these materials, once you apply them to your blank, the images/words will be in reverse.

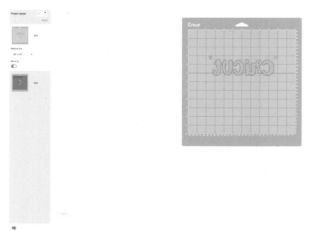

When you have a cutting mat selected, you also have the option of moving your design around anywhere you would like it to be on the mat. This feature comes in handy when you're using scrap pieces of cutting material, or when you're using your engraving tip to engrave on metal.

When you click on a design element on your cutting mat, you'll see a box appear around it with two different options:

1. **Three dots (. . .):** When you click on the "..." two options will come up. Move Object and Hide Object. When you click on the Move Object, it will give you the option to move your design to a different cutting mat. This can come in handy when you really want to make the most of your cutting material and pack as many cuts as possible into one mat. When you click Hide Object, that design will become hidden so that it no longer cuts.

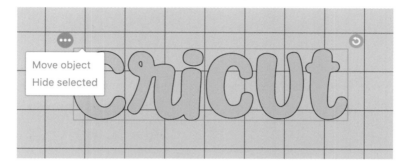

2. **Circle arrow:** The circle arrow will allow you to rotate your design. This feature comes in handy when you're trying to use up every last square inch of your cutting material.

Pro-Crafter Tip

I find I get the best cuts from my cutting machine if I'm very specific with the type of material I'm using, so I always leave my Cricut Explore Air dial set to Custom.

Once you have your designs placed on the cutting mat, you can click Continue. You will then be taken to a screen where you select your cutting machine and cutting material.

Your favorite cutting materials will appear on the screen. If you would like to pick a cutting material that is not shown, click Browse Materials. This will pull up a full list of cutting materials grouped by category. There is also a search box to make finding the material you're looking for easy.

If you discover once you get to this screen that you would like your design set on a different spot on the mat, or that you forgot to mirror your design, you can click on the Edit button under the cutting mat you would like to edit in the left-hand toolbar. It will pop up a larger view of your mat that you can rearrange. There is also a mirror slider at the bottom of this box so you can switch your design to be mirrored.

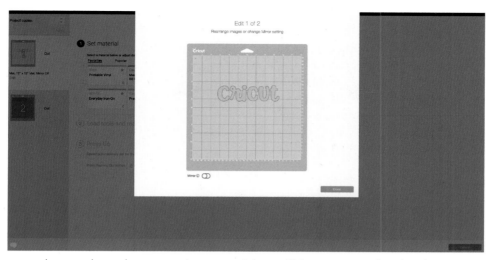

Once you have selected your cutting material, you'll be prompted to load any special blades, tools, or pens into your Cricut and to load your cutting mat into your machine.

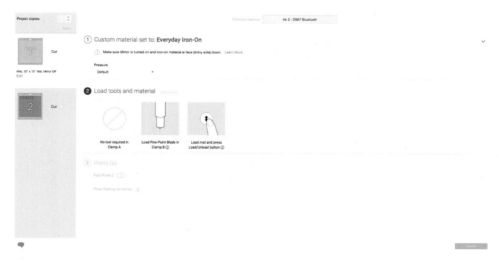

If you ever need to change the cutting material you have selected, simply click on the area that says Custom Material Set To and it will pull up the box where you can select a new cutting material.

SnapMat: Cricut has a feature that is available exclusively through their app on phones and tablets called SnapMat. When you use the SnapMat feature, it allows you to take a photo of your cutting mat with the material laid out and then position your cut wherever you would like it to be on the mat. I love using this feature when cutting fabric with a big, bold pattern. It allows me to "fussy cut," which means having your shape cut from a specific part of your fabric pattern.

And there you have it! Cricut Design Space 101! I hope that this served as a great walkthrough for you and that you learned about a tool or button or two you didn't know about in the past. The more you use Design Space, the more instinctual it will become, and before you know it, you'll be designing projects like a pro!

Downloading the Cut Files from This Book

This book comes with over thirty-five free cut files that you can download and use for personal use. To download the cut files, please visit hellocreativefamily.com/cricut-crafts-book-cut-files and enter the password: 56cr09ic23ut10cr89af45ts78.

I hope you love all the projects in this book. I would love to see the Cricut crafts that you make directly from this book, as well as the projects that this book inspires! Please tag @hellocreativefamily on Instagram and use the hashtag #HCFCricutCrafts. I also love hearing from you! Email me at crystal@hellocreativefamily.com to ask me your Cricut-related questions, show me your projects, and just to say hi!

40 Projects Using Cricut's Most Popular Materials

Now is when the fun really begins! Projects! You can make a million and one things with your Cricut cutting machine. My goal with this book is to give you ideas and skills that you can then transfer to create your own unique ideas. For example, I have a project on page 55 for a "Team Coffee" and "Team Tea" mugs. I would love for you to make a mug just like mine and show it to all your friends, but do you know what would give me even greater joy? If you took the skills that you learn making my mug and go on to make a bunch of other mugs for friends and family members with all kinds of *your* designs on them! That's where the possibilities become endless!

I've broken this chapter into 8 different materials:

- Vinyl
- Paper
- Heat Transfer Vinyl/Iron-On
- Fabric
- Basswood and Chipboard
- Leather and Faux Leather
- Infusible Ink
- Special Materials

You will find 4 to 6 projects for each material. For the iron-on, vinyl, and Infusible Ink, I've tried to use a wide variety of blanks (mugs, wood signs, clipboards, shirts, coasters, etc.) so that you really get to know how to use each material and how much you can do with them!

I've also put a list of tools and material suggestions at the beginning of each material category. These are tools that I use in my own craft room and love. They help take away frustration and make crafting life so much easier.

Are you ready to get crafting? Let's go!

An Introduction to Vinyl Projects

When I talk to people about what they plan on making with their new Cricut, they usually fall into one of three categories:

1. They want to vinyl all the things.
2. They want to make shirts using HTV or iron-on for every occasion.
3. They are card-makers and want to take their cards to the next level.

In this section, we're going to talk about vinyl. Vinyl is so much fun. If you loved stickers when you were a kid, you're going to love cutting vinyl with your Cricut. It's like making your very own stickers that you can put on just about anything!

Some ideas for vinyl projects:

- Mugs
- Water bottles
- Car/wall/laptop decals
- Cricut bling
- Wood signs
- Decorations picture frames
- Planner stickers

Vinyl comes in all different colors, patterns, and textures. There's glitter, holographic, matte, glossy, chalkboard, dry erase, and even glow-in-the-dark!

The number-one question you need to ask yourself when purchasing vinyl for a project is: How permanent do I want it to be?

Vinyl is available in four basic categories:

Permanent vinyl: Use this on anything that's going to be getting wet—whether that means washed with your dishes or outside in the elements. (Note: You can also get permanent outdoor vinyl, which is probably best to use for projects that will be exposed to rain, sun, and snow.) Perfect for glassware, mugs, shower doors, and more.

Removable vinyl: Removes without residue up to two years after being applied. I like to use removable vinyl on anything that isn't getting washed. Removable vinyl still has staying power, but if you need to peel it up for any reason, you can. It's fabulous for wall decals, indoor signs, decorating notebooks, putting quotes on mirrors, decorating your Cricut, and more.

Printable vinyl: Use Cricut's print-and-cut function combined with your home printer to print designs and then have your Cricut cut them. I love it for planner stickers, party decor, quick and easy custom crafts, and more. You can find one of my printable vinyl projects in the Special Materials section (page 247).

Heat transfer vinyl (also known as HTV or iron-on): Apply heat to this vinyl to get it to permanently adhere to fabric, paper, wood, and more. This type of vinyl is covered in a later chapter of this book (page 95).

Vinyl Lingo

Curious about the different terms people throw around when talking about Cricut crafts? We've got you covered!

Weeding: The process of removing the negative space around your design. So, for example, if you have your Cricut cut an "O," you would need to remove the excess vinyl from around the outside of your O and the inside of your O, leaving just the letter itself on the paper backing.

Print and Cut: A feature available in Cricut Design Space where you print a design using your home printer and then your Cricut cuts out the design for you.

Oracal 631: A brand of non-permanent vinyl that many professional crafters use. Matte finish. Ideal for wall decals, stencils, and other designs you may want to remove later.

Oracal 651: A brand of permanent vinyl that many professional crafters use. Glossy finish and outdoor safe. Ideal for mugs, permanent decals, and signs.

Burnish: The act of using a scraper or brayer tool to rub transfer tape laid over the top of the vinyl to help the vinyl stick to the surface.

Kiss cut: To cut through just the first layer of a material, not all the way through. A kiss cut is used with vinyl and HTV. It means that your machine will cut *only* the vinyl and not the paper backing. This is something that your Cricut will do for you automatically when set to the correct material setting.

Other Useful Tools & Materials for Working with Vinyl

- **Fine-tip cutting blade:** This is your go-to blade for cutting vinyl and most regular materials like iron-on, cardstock, scrapbook paper, and more. (See the materials list starting on page 5 for which blades you will need for different types of materials.)
- **Regular grip cutting mat:** A regular grip cutting mat has the perfect grip for keeping your vinyl secure while cutting and then releasing your vinyl without disturbing the design.
- **Transfer tape:** The transfer tape I use comes in regular grip, which is appropriate for most vinyl, and StrongGrip, which is best for "specialty" vinyl like glitter and shimmer. Transfer tape is used to transfer your vinyl from the paper backing it comes on to wherever you will be placing it. I like using clear transfer tape with a grid pattern so I can see exactly where I am placing my design and can make sure it's lined up properly.
- **Weeding tools:** Weeding tools help you remove the extra vinyl and are especially helpful when weeding small letters and intricate designs. You also use weeding tools with HTV.
- **Cricut Bright Pad:** If your eyes aren't what they once were, then a Cricut Bright Pad is a big help. It looks like a large iPad with a variety of light settings. Lay your vinyl over the top of the Bright Pad and your cut lines will become illuminated, making weeding much easier.
- **Scraper or brayer tools:** A scraper or brayer tool is especially handy when working with vinyl. It's used to help your vinyl stick to the transfer tape and then to your project. If you're in a pinch, an old credit card can do the job of a scraper or brayer when transferring vinyl, too.

#CREATIVE CRICUT BLING

Cricut Explore **or** Cricut Maker Project (Cricut Joy Compatible)

Give your Cricut a bit of bling with this fun project! One of the very first projects many Cricut crafters do when they get a new cutting machine is pick a word or design and cut a decal to place on their machine. My very first Cricut said "Sew Creative," which was the name of my blog at the time. My Cricut Maker has a decal with my logo in pink and teal sparkle. I thought it was only fitting to start this book with a bit of Cricut bling! I believe with my heart and soul that the Cricut cutting machine will turn anyone into a creative, so I decided to create a #Creative design. If #Creative isn't your cup of tea, then think of a word or design that feels fitting for your new machine! Then visit Design Space, play around with some fonts, and design your very own Cricut bling! I'd love to see your machine decorated! Share a picture on Instagram using the hashtag **#hcfcricutcrafts** and tag **@hellocreativefamily!**

Materials:

- #Creative cut file
- Measuring tape
- Vinyl in your favorite color
- Regular grip cutting mat
- Fine-tip blade
- Weeding tools
- Transfer tape
- Scraper tool

Directions:

Step 1: Log into Cricut Design Space and upload the #Creative cut file following the Cut File Upload instructions on page 28 of this book.

Step 2: Measure the space on your Cricut where you want to place your bling. Size your design accordingly by clicking on the design and using either the arrow that appears in the bottom right-hand corner of the design or the Size tool in the top toolbar.

Step 2.

Step 3: Click **Make It**. Set your cutting material to the type of vinyl you're using. Lay vinyl on your cutting mat with the color side facing up. Load your cutting mat into your Cricut using the arrow on the right-hand side of your Cricut. Once your mat is loaded, look for the Cricut C to start flashing, press the button, and your machine will start cutting. When your machine finishes cutting, press the arrow again and your mat will unload.

Step 3.

Step 4: Weed your vinyl, removing the excess vinyl around your design, leaving just the design on the white paper backing.

Step 4.

Step 5: Cut a piece of transfer tape a tiny bit bigger than your design. Peel the tape off the backing and lay it on the top of your design. Use your scraper tool to rub over top of the transfer tape, pushing the tape against the vinyl. Peel the transfer tape up, lifting your vinyl design away from the paper backing.

Step 6: Position your transfer tape so that the sticky back of the vinyl is where you would like your design placed. Run your scraper tool over the top of the transfer tape, pushing it against your Cricut so it's firmly adhered. Carefully lift your transfer tape, leaving just your design behind!

Congratulations! You have some awesome Cricut bling! Every time you use your machine, you'll remember your very first project!

Step 5.

Step 6.

Step 5.

Finished project.

"TEAM COFFEE" AND "TEAM TEA" MUGS

Cricut Explore **or** Cricut Maker Project (Cricut Joy Compatible)

Are you Team Coffee or Team Tea? Whichever team you're on, mugs make a great beginner Cricut project! It's super fun to have a one-of-a-kind mug that is a reflection of your personality. Mugs also make an excellent handmade gift! I'm providing you with cut files to make either a tea mug or a coffee mug, but once you've made this project, I highly suggest you let your imagination run wild and really customize the mugs you make as gifts! Does the recipient have a favorite hobby? Love a certain breed of dog? Are they a grandma, uncle, or the best friend in the whole world? Are they truly passionate about their profession? Those are just a few jumping-off points to think about when designing your future mugs!

Materials:
- Coffee and Tea Cut Files
- Mugs
- Measuring tape
- Permanent vinyl in your favorite color
- Regular grip cutting mat
- Fine-tip blade
- Weeding tools
- Transfer tape
- Scraper tool

Directions:

Step 1: Log into Cricut Design Space and upload the Coffee and Tea cut files following the Cut File Upload instructions on page 28 of this book.

Step 2: Measure the space on your mugs where you want to place your bling. Size your design accordingly by clicking on the design and using either the arrow that appears in the bottom right-hand corner of the design or the Size tool in the top toolbar.

Step 2.

Step 3: Click **Make It**. Set your cutting material to the type of vinyl you're using. Lay vinyl on your cutting mat with the color side facing up. Load your cutting mat into your Cricut using the arrow on the right-hand side of your Cricut. Once your mat is loaded, look for the Cricut C to start flashing, press the button, and your machine will start cutting. When your machine

finishes cutting, press the arrow again and your mat will unload.

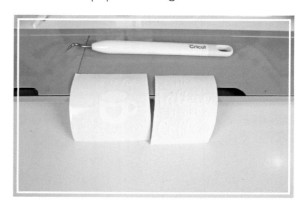

Step 3.

Step 4: Weed your vinyl, removing the excess vinyl around your design, leaving just the design on the white paper backing.

Step 4.

Step 5: Cut a piece of transfer tape a tiny bit bigger than your design. Peel the tape off the backing and lay it on top of your design. Use your scraper tool to rub over the top of the transfer tape, pushing the tape against the vinyl. Peel the transfer tape up, lifting your vinyl design away from the paper backing.

Step 5.

Step 6: Carefully position and then lay the transfer tape onto your mug. Run your scraper over the transfer tape, pushing the vinyl onto the mug. Carefully peel away the transfer tape, leaving the design on your mug. If the vinyl starts to lift, use your scraper to push it down, then peel the transfer tape away again.

Allow the vinyl on your mug to cure for 48 hours and then you can start using it! I suggest handwashing your mug for longevity of the vinyl! Proudly show the world whether you are Team Coffee or Team Tea every time you use your pretty new mug!

Pro-Crafter Tip

Putting vinyl onto a curved surface like a mug can be tricky to do without getting bubbles. I have two tips to make it easier.

1. Keep your designs small. You're going to have much more luck putting something like a font that has "white space" between the letters on a mug than a big piece of solid vinyl that will get wrinkles in it as it lays around the curve.

2. Cut snips every ¼ to ½ inch all the way around the outside edge of your transfer tape, making sure to not cut your design. This will let your transfer tape have more flexibility and let your vinyl lay down nicely.

Step 6.

"Dream Big" Color Block Clipboard

Cricut Explore **or** Cricut Maker Project

I'm always on the lookout for blank "things" that I can decorate with my Cricut. Clipboards are one of my favorites! The first clipboards I put vinyl designs on were for my kids in preparation for a big road trip we had planned. I printed out coloring sheets, word searches, and other fun paper activities that would keep them entertained during our long trip. I have also given a ton of clipboards as teacher gifts! I decorate the board with a fun inspirational quote and clip a gift card to it for an easy handmade gift that has a fabulous sentiment to it.

This clipboard I made for my own office. I clip my editorial calendar to it, along with daily, weekly, monthly, and yearly goals. It helps keep me on track and always reminds me to dream big!

Materials:

- Dream Big Clipboard Cut File
- Measuring tape
- Clipboard
- Vinyl in 2 of your favorite colors
- Regular grip cutting mat
- Fine-tip blade
- Weeding tools
- Transfer tape
- Scraper tool or braying tool

Directions:

Step 1: Log into Cricut Design Space and upload the Dream Big Clipboard cut file following the SVG Upload instructions on page 22 of this book.

Step 2: Measure the width of your clipboard and size your design accordingly. Do this by clicking on the design and using either the arrow that appears in the bottom right-hand corner of the design or use the Size tool in the top toolbar.

Step 3.

Step 4: Weed your vinyl, removing the excess vinyl around your design and leaving only the designs on the white paper backing.

Step 2.

Step 3: Click Make It. Set your cutting material to the type of vinyl you're using. Lay vinyl on your cutting mat with the color side facing up. Load your cutting mat into your Cricut using the arrow on the right-hand side of your Cricut. Once your mat is loaded, look for the Cricut C to start flashing, press the button, and your machine will start cutting. When your machine finishes cutting, press the arrow again and your mat will unload. Repeat this step with the second piece of your design.

Step 4.

Step 5: Cut a piece of transfer tape a tiny bit bigger than your large color block piece. Peel the tape off the backing of the transfer tape and lay it on top of your design. Use your scraper tool or brayer to rub over the top of the transfer tape, pushing the tape against the vinyl. Peel the transfer tape up, lifting your vinyl design away from the paper backing.

Step 5.

Step 6: Carefully position and then lay the transfer tape onto your clipboard. Run your scraper over the transfer tape, pushing the vinyl onto the clipboard. Carefully peel away the transfer tape, leaving the design on your clipboard. If the vinyl starts to lift, use your scraper to push it down then peel the transfer tape away again. Repeat steps 5 and 6 with the Dream Big words.

Step 6.

Use your new clipboard to keep track of goals, to-do lists, and other special notes that will help you get closer to your big dream each day!

"Be-you-tiful" Wood Watercolor Picture Frame

The wood aisle is one of my very favorite sections to visit at the craft store. Once you own a Cricut, everywhere you go, you're looking for blank canvases to Cricut on, and the wood aisle has some great options. I'm always on the lookout for wood picture frames to decorate with my Cricut. I especially love them as a Cricut craft for kids, tweens, and teens. I love seeing each young artist's personality shine through with the way they paint their picture frame and the word or design they choose for the vinyl. I chose the quote "Be-you-tiful" for this project because I think it's a message that many young girls and boys need to hear more.

Materials:

- Wood picture frame
- Paint (I used watercolor paint for this project)
- Paint brushes
- Be-you-tiful cut file
- Measuring tape
- Vinyl (I used white and pink)
- Regular grip cutting mat
- Fine-tip blade
- Weeding tools
- Transfer tape
- Scraper tool or braying tool

Directions:

Step 1: Paint your picture frame. Allow the frame to thoroughly dry before attempting to apply vinyl to it.

Step 1.

Step 2: Log into Cricut Design Space and upload the Be-you-tiful cut file following the Cut File Upload instructions on page 28 of this book.

Step 3: Measure the space where you will be applying your vinyl to your picture frame and size your design accordingly. Do this by clicking on the design and using either the arrow that appears in the bottom right-hand corner of the design or the **Size** tool in the top toolbar.

Step 3.

Step 4: Click **Make It**. Set your cutting material to the type of vinyl you're using. Lay vinyl on your cutting mat with the color side facing up. Load your cutting mat into your Cricut using the arrow on the right-hand side of your Cricut. Once your mat is loaded, look for the Cricut C to start flashing, press the button, and your machine will start cutting. When your machine finishes cutting, press the arrow again and your mat will unload. Repeat this step with the second piece of your design.

Step 4.

Step 5: Weed your vinyl, removing the excess vinyl around your design and leaving just the designs on the white paper backing.

Step 5.

Step 6: Cut a piece of transfer tape a tiny bit bigger than your design. Peel the tape off the backing of the transfer tape and lay it on top of your design. Use your scraper tool or brayer to rub over the top of the transfer tape, pushing the tape against the vinyl. Peel the transfer tape up, lifting your vinyl design away from the paper backing.

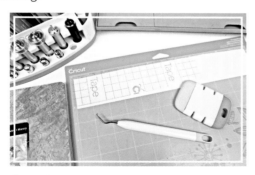

Step 6.

Step 7: Carefully position and then lay the transfer tape onto your picture frame where you would like your design to be. Run your scraper over the transfer tape, pushing the vinyl onto the picture frame. Carefully peel away the transfer tape, leaving the design.

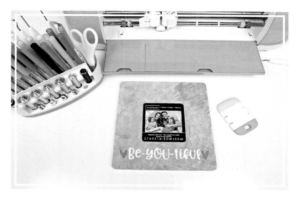

Step 7.

Give this picture frame as a gift to someone in your life who needs a reminder of how "be-you-tiful" they are. Don't forget to put a picture of them you love in the frame!

Vinyl Scrap Nail Decals

Cricut Explore **or** Cricut Maker Project (Cricut Joy Compatible)

What's a crafty girl supposed to do with all her teeny-tiny leftover vinyl scraps? Why, make vinyl nail decals, of course! As the mother of a tweenage daughter, nails are a very big deal in my house. My daughter and I love sitting at the table together, listening to music, chatting, and giving ourselves manicures. As an avid Cricut crafter, I have a ton of tiny vinyl scraps laying around in my craft room, and pretty little nail decals are a great way to use them up. I love doing my nail decals in simple shapes like hearts, polka-dots, and stars. Because the stickers are being cut in such a small size, the less intricate the design, the better (it also makes it easier to keep the decal adhered to your nail). Have fun playing with different designs and color combinations! Make sure to share your pretty Cricut nails with me on Instagram by using the hashtag **#HCFCricutCrafts** and tagging **@hellocreativefamily**.

Materials:

- Vinyl scraps (I used some holographic sparkle vinyl for a bit of extra bling)
- Regular grip cutting mat
- Fine-tip blade
- Clear nail polish

Directions:

Step 1: Log into Cricut Design Space and choose a shape. Hearts, stars, circles, and other simple shapes can be found free to use under the **Shape** tool. Size your shape as desired for your nail decals. I suggest between 0.15 inches to 0.5 inches, depending on the size of your nail.

Step 2: Click **Make It**. Set your cutting material to the type of vinyl you're using. Lay vinyl on your cutting mat with the color side facing up. Load your cutting mat into your Cricut using the arrow on the right-hand side of your Cricut. Once your mat is loaded, look for the Cricut C to start flashing, press the button, and your machine will start cutting. When your machine finishes cutting, press the arrow again and your mat will unload.

Step 3: Weed your vinyl, removing the excess vinyl around your design and leaving just the design on the white paper backing.

Step 4: Carefully peel your decals from the paper backing and apply them to your nails. Apply a layer of clear nail polish over the top of your decals to give them staying power!

There you go! You have the cutest, craftiest nails around! Create a bunch of nail decals in different sizes, shapes, and colors and have a manicure party with your crafty besties!

Step 1.

Step 2.

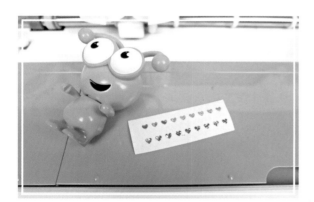

Step 3.

Step 4.

An Introduction to Paper Projects

Let's Talk Paper!

Paper is a fabulous material to start with when you are first learning how to use your Cricut because it's one of the least expensive materials you can buy. A lot of card-makers buy Cricuts to help bring their card-making skills to the next level, never expecting that it will open up a world of possibilities for the rest of their crafting life!

Some ideas for paper projects:

- Cards
- Gift tags
- Paper flowers
- Paper succulents
- Planner accessories

- Luminaries
- Shadowbox art
- Bookmarks
- Scrapbooking embellishments

The Cricut can cut paper in all different thicknesses, finishes, and weights. You can see a full list of the types of paper that the Cricut Maker and Cricut Explore can cut at the beginning of this book (page 5).

Some of my favorite paper projects have used these types of paper:

- Glitter cardstock
- Scrapbook paper
- Regular cardstock
- Crepe paper
- Vellum
- Cereal boxes

- Construction paper
- Poster board
- Freezer paper
- Photographs

Paper Lingo

Curious about the different terms people are throwing around when talking about Cricut Crafts? We've got you covered!

Paper Weight: When cutting cardstock with your Cricut Maker or on the custom setting on the Cricut Explore, you'll have to choose which weight of paper you're using. Paper weight refers to how much 500 sheets of the paper in their original, uncut form (before it's cut to 8.5 x 11 or 12 x 12) weigh.

Weeding: The process of removing the negative space around your design, leaving your design on the cutting mat.

Print and Cut: A feature available in Cricut Design Space where you print a design using your home printer and then your Cricut cuts out the design for you.

Scoring: Creating an indentation in the paper, usually in the form of a line, so your paper will fold cleanly and easily along the crease.

Quilling: Winding paper around a quill to create a coil shape.

> **Pro-Crafter Tip**
> When removing your paper from the cutting mat, gently bend the mat to remove the paper instead of pulling the paper straight off the mat. This will help keep your paper from curling during the removal process.

Other Useful Tools & Materials for Working with Paper

1. **Fine-tip cutting blade:** This is your go-to blade for cutting paper and most regular materials like iron-on, cardstock, scrapbook paper, and more. (See the materials list at the beginning of the book for which blades you will need for different types of materials.)
2. **LightGrip cutting mat:** A LightGrip cutting mat has the perfect grip for keeping your paper secure while cutting and not tearing your paper when trying to remove it from your mat.
3. **Weeding tools:** Weeding tools help you remove the negative space from around your design. This would be especially helpful with paper when doing more intricate designs like for shadowboxes, for example.
4. **Brayer tools:** I love using a brayer to evenly push the paper down onto the LightGrip cutting mat, so there's no risk of the paper shifting while cutting.
5. **Quilling tool:** This tool comes in handy anytime you have to roll paper tightly. I love it for making paper flowers and succulents.

"HANDMADE WITH LOVE" &
"THANK YOU" GIFT TAGS

Cricut Maker **or** Cricut Explore Project

Once you own a Cricut, you'll discover that there are so many things you're used to buying that you can now make—like gift tags! Use your Cricut to cut pretty, colored cardstock, scrapbook paper, outdated calendars, old cards, and other paper to make beautiful gift tags! Or use plain white cardstock and Cricut's Print and Cut feature—like we're going to do in this project—to create a power duo between your Cricut and your printer!

Materials:

- "Handmade With Love" and "Thank You" Gift Tag Cut File
- White cardstock
- Color printer
- LightGrip cutting mat
- Fine-tip blade

Directions:

Step 1: Log into Cricut Design Space and upload the gift tags cut file following the Cut File Upload instructions on page 28 of this book.

Step 2: Size your design so it is 9.25 inches on its widest side by clicking on the design and using either the arrow that appears in the bottom right-hand corner of the design or the Size tool in the top toolbar.

Step 3: Click Make It. Follow the prompts on the screen. First, you'll print your gift tags using your printer. Then you'll select your cutting material, place your printed gift tags on the cutting mat, and load it into the machine using the arrow button on the right-hand side of the machine. Once your mat is loaded, look for the Cricut C to start flashing, press the button, and your machine will start cutting. When your machine finishes cutting, press the arrow again and your mat will unload.

Step 2.

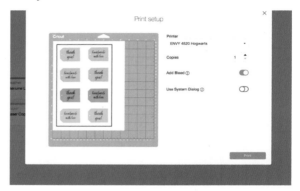

Step 3.

Step 3.

Note: Don't be alarmed if your Cricut doesn't start cutting immediately. You will probably notice a light turn on near the blade. The mat will move as the light scans back and forth across your paper. This is your Cricut looking for the black border so it knows where to cut.

Step 4: Carefully remove your gift tags from the cutting mat. They're ready to use!

Step 4.

Enjoy your beautiful gift tags! What other ways can you think of to use your Cricut to decorate gifts?

Pro-Crafter Tip
Finding you get a curl in your paper every time you remove it from the cutting mat? Try gently curling your cutting mat to remove the paper, instead of curling your paper to remove it from the mat!

Finished project.

SLEEPY VILLAGE LUMINARIES

Cricut Maker **or** Cricut Explore Project (Cricut Joy Compatible)

Create a beautiful, glowing, winter wonderland with these easy-to-make house luminaries. Lit with a battery-operated candle, these paper houses create a beautiful effect for any mantle or as a table centerpiece. Use one cut file to make houses in a variety of sizes and colors to create the tiny village of your dreams!

Materials:

- Sleepy Village Cut File
- Cardstock in a variety of sizes and colors (We used 8.5 x 11, 12 x 12, and 12 x 24 for our luminaries)
- LightGrip cutting mat
- Fine-tip blade
- Scoring stylus or scoring wheel
- Glue or Glue Dots
- Battery-operated candles

Directions:

Step 1: Log into Cricut Design Space and upload the Sleepy Village cut file following the Cut File Upload instructions on page 28 of this book.

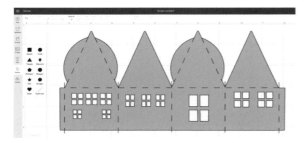

Step 1.

Step 2: Click the Shapes button in the right-hand toolbar and select the score line. Add score lines to all the places indicated in the photo. These are all the places that you will want your paper to be able to fold to make your houses. Once you have all your score lines placed where you want them, select the house and all the score lines and click Attach.

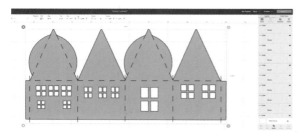

Step 2.

Step 3: Click the Duplicate button to create as many houses as desired. Click the Lock button to unlock the size proportion. Play with the house sizes, making some taller and skinnier, some shorter and wider, some bigger and some smaller. Make sure to pay attention to what size cutting mats and paper you have so each house will fit on your paper.

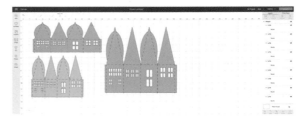

Step 3.

Step 4: Click Make It. Follow the prompts on the screen. Lay cardstock on your cutting mat and put your scoring stylus or scoring wheel into your machine. Load your mat into the machine using the arrow button on the right-hand side of the machine. Once your mat is loaded, look for the Cricut C to start flashing, press the button, and your machine will start scoring and cutting. When your machine finishes cutting, press the arrow again and your mat will unload.

Step 4.

Step 5: Once you have all your houses cut, fold your cardstock at each score line. Use Glue Dots or glue to hold the tabs in place.

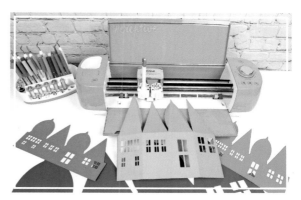

Step 5.

Place one or more battery-operated candles inside each house and create your own beautiful, glowing, sleepy village!

KAWAII FOOD MAGNETIC BOOKMARKS

Cricut Maker **or** Cricut Explore Project

I come from a family of very big readers. My husband and I met while working at a bookstore and later both went on to work at the same publishing company. My daughter is a voracious reader and carries a stack of books with her wherever she goes. My son has just recently learned to read and is definitely following in his sister's footsteps as a child who can't get enough books. I created the idea of these magnetic bookmarks after getting tired of seeing books laid open on tables, the couch, and just about every single other surface of my house! Fold the bookmark over the page where you've left off and the magnetic closer will attach to the backside of the page, marking your spot securely! These magnetic bookmarks make the sweetest little handmade gifts! We have given them as stocking stuffers, gifts for friends, and have even sold them at our local craft fair!

Materials:

- Kawaii Food Magnetic Bookmarks Cut File
- White 8.5 x 11-inch cardstock
- Color printer
- LightGrip cutting mat
- Fine-tip blade
- Scoring blade or scoring stylus
- Magnetic sticker paper
- Scissors

Directions:

Step 1: Log into Cricut Design Space and upload the Kawaii food cut files following the Cut File Upload instructions on page 28 of this book.

Step 2: Size each bookmark as desired by clicking on the design and using either the arrow that appears in the bottom right-hand corner of the design or the Size tool in the top toolbar. Our bookmarks were 6 inches long.

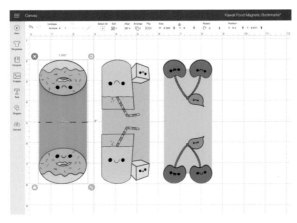

Step 2.

Step 3: Add score lines to your bookmark. Click on the Shapes button in the left-hand toolbar. Select the score line. Rotate the score line by 90 degrees. Lay the score line on top of each bookmark, then select both the bookmark and the score line and click the Center Vertically option under the align button. With both the score line and bookmark selected, click the Attach button. Repeat for each bookmark.

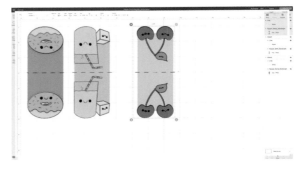

Step 3.

Step 4: Click Make It. Follow the prompts on the screen. First, you'll print your bookmarks on the cardstock using your printer. Then you'll select your cutting material, place your printed page on the cutting mat, and load it into the machine using the arrow button on the right-hand side of the machine. Once your mat is loaded, look for the Cricut C to start flashing, press the button, and your machine will start cutting. When your machine finishes cutting, press the arrow again and your mat will unload.

Step 4.

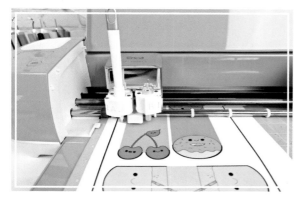

Step 4.

Note: Don't be alarmed if your Cricut doesn't start cutting immediately. You will probably notice a light turn on near the blade. The mat will move as the light scans back and forth across your paper. This is your Cricut looking for the black border so that it knows where to cut.

Step 5: Carefully remove your bookmarks from the cutting mat and fold each one on the score line. Cut two squares of magnets from your magnetic sticker sheet and stick the magnets on the inside (non-printed side) of the bookmarks so the two magnets are lined up.

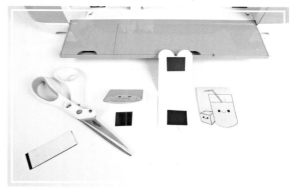

Step 5.

Slip over the page of a book and mark your place with these adorable Kawaii food bookmarks!

FATHER'S DAY AND MOTHER'S DAY PHOTO CARDS

Cricut Maker **or** Cricut Explore Project

I love incorporating photos into hand-made gifts. I love how many special memories photos hold and how one look at a photo can take you right back to a specific time or place. This project is to teach you how to make a photo card and envelope. I've included elements to turn this into a Mother's Day or Father's Day card. Once you know the basics, you can use this cut file to make photo cards for any holiday or special occasion by adding your own extra embellishments. Photo cards are great for Christmas, Valentine's Day, anniversaries, birthdays, graduation, baby shower thank-you cards, and more!

Materials:

- Photo card cut file
- Envelope cut file
- Mother's Day embellishment Print and Cut File
- Father's Day embellishment Print and Cut File
- White 8.5 x 11-inch cardstock
- 3 pieces 12 x 12-inch cardstock in your favorite colors or patterns
- Color printer
- LightGrip cutting mat
- Fine-tip blade
- Scoring blade or scoring stylus
- Glue Dots
- Your favorite photo

Directions:

Step 1: Log into Cricut Design Space and upload the photo card, envelope, and Mother's Day or Father's Day cut files following the Cut File Upload instructions on page 28 of this book. Make sure to save Mother's Day elements and Father's Day elements as a Print and Cut image.

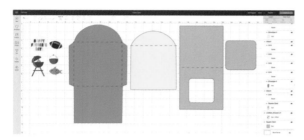

Step 1.

Step 2: Size the card so that it's 5 inches wide. Size the square photo backer with rounded corners so that it's 4 inches wide. Size the envelope so that it's 11.75 inches tall. Size the Mother's Day and Father's Day elements to desired sizes for decorating your card.

Step 3: Use the **Detach** button in the right-hand toolbar to detach your envelope and the envelope liner. Add score lines to the envelope, envelope liner, and card. To add a score line, click on the **Shapes** button in the left-hand toolbar. Select the Score Line. Lay the score where you would like it on the card or envelope then select both the score line and what you are attaching it to and click the **Attach** button from the right-hand side toolbar. For the card, you may like to use the **Align** button in the upper toolbar to center your score line on the card.

Step 4: Click **Make It**. Follow the prompts on the screen. First, you'll print your Mother's Day or Father's Day elements using your printer. Then you'll select your cutting material, place your printed pages on the cutting mat, and load it into the machine using the arrow button on the right-hand side of the machine. Once your mat is loaded, look for the Cricut C to start flashing, press the button, and your machine will start cutting. When your machine finishes cutting, press the arrow again and your mat will unload.

Step 4.

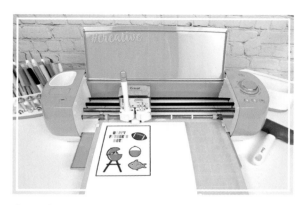

Step 4.

Note: Don't be alarmed if your Cricut doesn't start cutting immediately. You will probably notice a light turn on near the blade. The mat will move as the light scans back and forth across your paper. This is your Cricut looking for the black border so it knows where to cut.

Step 5: Once all your pieces have been cut, fold each piece with a score line along the score line. Next, use Glue Dots to attach the envelope liner to the inside of the envelope, then glue the flaps of the envelope shut. Then, attach your Father's Day or Mother's Day elements to the front of your card. Finally, stick a photo inside the hole of the card and use Glue Dots to affix the photo backer to seal your photo in place.

Step 5.

Now you have a beautiful photo card for Mother's Day or Father's Day! Personalize the card even further by using elements for the front of the card that are related to hobbies or things the recipient is interested in.

Pom-Pom Party Hats

Cricut Maker **or** Cricut Explore Project

Party planning is so much more fun when you own a Cricut because you can customize EVERYTHING! On page 105 of this book, I show you how to decorate paper napkins using iron-on. In this project, I'm sharing how to make easy party hats that you can top with a pom-pom or felt ball! There are so many options of scrapbook paper at the craft store in all kinds of colors and designs, so the possibilities really are endless with these. Can't find a design you like? Pick a fun color of scrapbook paper, cut out iron-on or vinyl in shapes that fit your theme, and adhere them to the scrapbook paper before assembling them into party hats!

Materials:

- Party hat cut file
- LightGrip cutting mat
- 12 x 12-inch scrapbook paper in fun colors and designs (1 piece per hat)
- Fine-tip blade
- Glue gun and hot glue sticks
- Pom-poms or felt balls
- Hole punch
- Yarn, string, or elastic
- Scissors
- Optional: Brayer (I like this for pushing the paper onto the fine grip cutting mat to make sure it doesn't slide.)

Directions:

Step 1: Log into Cricut Design Space and upload the Party Hat cut file following the Cut File Upload instructions on page 28 of this book.

Step 2: Size the cut file so that it is 11.5 inches wide. You can do this by clicking on the image and using either the sizing arrow or the sizing boxes in the toolbar at the top of Cricut Design Space.

Step 3: Click Make It. Follow the prompts on the screen. Select your cutting material, place your scrapbook paper on the cutting mat, and load it into the machine using the arrow button on the right-hand side of the machine. Once your mat is loaded, look for the Cricut C to start flashing, press the button, and your machine will start cutting. When your machine finishes cutting, press the arrow again and your mat will unload.

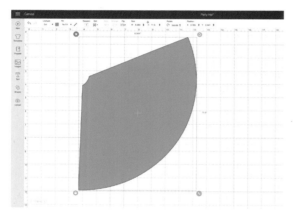

Step 2.

Step 3.

Step 4: Carefully remove the scrapbook paper from the cutting mat. Roll the scrapbook into the shape of a party hat, then apply hot glue to the edge of the paper where it overlaps, sealing it closed. Apply a bead of hot glue to your pom-pom or felt ball and apply it to the top of the hat.

Step 5: Use your hole punch to create holes near the bottom on both sides of your party hat. Cut pieces of yarn, string, or elastic in the appropriate sizes for chin straps for your party guests. Tie the yarn through the holes that you've just punched, creating chin straps.

Step 5.

Have tons of festive fun wearing your party hats at your next big celebration! What other ways could you customize party decor using your Cricut?

Step 4.

An Introduction to Heat Transfer Vinyl (HTV) and Iron-On

Let's Talk HTV!

I'll confess—HTV is my very favorite cutting material. Many people consult me when trying to decide if they will use their Cricut enough for it to be worth the cost. In my mind, being able to make your own custom shirts makes the price of a Cricut well worth it! HTV can be applied to so much more than just shirts, though!

What can you adhere HTV to?

- Clothing
- Hats
- Swimwear
- Neoprene
- Paper
- Burlap
- Wood
- Fabric

- Canvas
- Chipboard
- Corkboard
- Faux Leather
- Leather
- Felt
- Wool
- And more!

What's in a name?

Heat transfer vinyl, HTV, iron-on—they're all different words for the same material! The terms can be used interchangeably, so don't get confused if you hear a crafter hopping from one term to another.

HTV comes in a ton of great styles, colors, patterns, and finishes. Some of my favorites are:

- Everyday Iron-On
- Holographic Iron-On
- Foil Iron-On
- Flocked Iron-On
- Glow-in-the-Dark Iron-On
- SportsFlex Iron-On
- Patterned Iron-On
- Mesh Iron-On
- Mosaic Iron-On
- Glitter Iron-On

HTV Lingo

Curious about the different terms people throw around when talking about Cricut Crafts? We've got you covered!

Weeding: The process of removing the negative space around your design. So, for example, if you have your Cricut cut an "O," you would need to remove the excess HTV from around the outside of your O and the inside of your O, leaving just the letter itself on the plastic backing.

Mirror: To flip or reverse an image. You do this when cutting a design out of heat transfer vinyl (HTV) because you cut the HTV with the back side facing up on your cutting mat.

Kiss cut: To cut through just the first layer of a material, not all the way through. A kiss cut is used with HTV and vinyl. It means that your machine will just cut the HTV and not the plastic backing. This is something that your Cricut will do automatically for you when set to the correct material setting.

Heat Press: A machine used to heat your HTV and make it adhere to the material you're attaching it to.

Other Useful Tools & Materials for Working with HTV

- **Fine-tip cutting blade:** This is your go-to blade for cutting HTV and most regular materials like vinyl, cardstock, scrapbook paper, and more. (See the materials list at the beginning of the book for which blades you will need for different types of materials, page 7).
- **Regular grip cutting mat:** A regular grip cutting mat has the perfect grip for keeping your HTV secure while cutting.
- **Weeding tools:** Weeding tools help you remove the "negative space" HTV from in and around your design. It's especially helpful when weeding small letters and intricate designs. You also use weeding tools with vinyl and paper.
- **Cricut Bright Pad:** If your eyes aren't what they once were, then a Cricut Bright Pad is a big help. It looks like a large iPad with a variety of light settings. Lay your HTV over the top of the Bright Pad and your cut lines will become illuminated, making weeding much easier.
- **Brayer tools:** Having a brayer tool is especially handy when working with HTV. I love rolling my brayer over the top of my design between each press. I find that it really helps ensure that my HTV is pressed into and sticking to the fibers of whatever I'm adhering it to.
- **Iron-On Protective Sheet:** Made with a nonstick surface, iron-on protective sheets help protect your HTV from getting damaged by heat. They also help distribute the heat from your EasyPress, heat press, or iron more evenly.
- **Cricut EasyPress or Heat Press:** The Cricut EasyPress is available in four sizes, all the way from an itty bitty EasyPress Mini to a 12 x 10–inch press that's perfect for larger designs. Heat presses and EasyPresses have even heat signatures, precise temperature control, and an even pressure that helps you get flawless results.
- **EasyPress Mat:** This handy little mat isn't just for protecting your work surface from heat (though it does that, too!). It has a special inner liner that wicks moisture to deliver clean, dry heat and a foil membrane that reflects heat to your project. The soft protective barrier bottom also helps seal layers together for beautiful HTV results!

CRAFTY SWEATSHIRT

Cricut Explore or Cricut Maker Project (Cricut Joy Compatible)

Do you have a favorite sweatshirt? An adorable sweatshirt is a must in my wardrobe. I snuggle up in them with a cup of tea at my desk while I'm working. I throw it on over a pair of leggings with a colorful scarf when picking up my kids from school. I wear it with some cute accessories and a pair of knee-high boots when going out with friends. I'm definitely a comfy sweatshirt kind of girl. My old favorite sweatshirt has officially gone into retirement after making my new Crafty Sweatshirt! It combines three of my favorite things: cute comfort, bright rainbow colors, and crafting! Head to the store, pick up a blank sweatshirt that you love, and make one of your own! Not a fan of sweatshirts? Make this on a tank top, T-shirt, or even on a tote bag that you put craft supplies in!

Materials:

- Crafty cut file
- Measuring tape
- Blank sweatshirt
- Heat transfer vinyl in your favorite colors
- Regular grip cutting mat
- Fine-tip blade
- Weeding tools
- Cricut EasyPress or Iron
- EasyPress Mat or a towel to protect your work surface
- Optional: Brayer and iron-on protective sheet

Directions:

Step 1: Log into Cricut Design Space and upload the "Crafty" cut file following the Cut File Upload instructions on page 28 of this book. Click on each piece of the cut file and change it to the color of HTV you will be using.

Step 2: Measure where you want the design to be on your sweatshirt. Size your design by clicking on it and using either the arrow that appears in the bottom right-hand corner of the design or the Size tool in the top toolbar.

Step 2.

Pro-Crafter HTV Tip

Click the button in Design Space that says **Templates**. A menu will pop up with a bunch of different items that you might want to Cricut on. Pick the one that looks the most like the blank you're using and see how your design looks on that object before cutting it out.

Step 3: Click Make It. Click the mirror slider under each cutting mat on the left-hand side of the screen. Set your cutting material to the type of HTV you're using and follow the prompts on the screen. Lay your iron-on with the color side down on the cutting mat then load your cutting mat into the machine using the arrow on the right-hand side of your Cricut. Once your mat is loaded, look for the Cricut C to start flashing, press the button, and your machine will start cutting. When your machine finishes cutting, press the arrow again and your mat will unload. Repeat with each color of HTV.

Step 4: Weed your HTV, removing the material around your design, leaving just the design on the clear plastic backing.

Step 4.

Step 3.

Step 5: Trim away the majority of the clear plastic backing around your letters so you can lay your design on the sweatshirt without anything overlapping. Follow the instructions for applying the type of iron-on you're using to the material that your sweatshirt is made from.

Step 5.

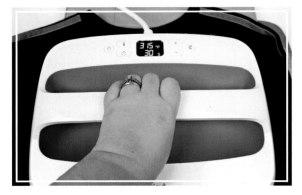

Step 5.

Optional: Use the iron-on protective sheet to give an extra layer of protection to your design. I also love to use the brayer tool with HTV to really push the vinyl into the fibers of the shirt between each press.

Step 6: Carefully peel up the clear plastic liner and reveal your brand-new crafty sweatshirt!

Rock your crafty persona! Take a picture of yourself out and about wearing your new sweatshirt and use the hashtag **#hcfcricutcrafts** and tag **@hellocreativefamily** on Instagram!

"CELEBRATE" NAPKINS

Cricut Maker **or** Cricut Explore Project (Cricut Joy Compatible)

Planning a party or other celebration? Applying HTV to paper napkins is a great way to take store-bought paper napkins to a whole new level! Personalize napkins with initials or a monogram for weddings, cut a design in the shape of your party theme, add a number for a birthday, or just use the word *Celebrate* for any festive occasion. This project is so simple and fun, and you'll get a ton of use out of it! Put on your thinking cap and come up with ideas for Christmas, New Year's Eve, Easter, Fourth of July, Mother's Day, Father's Day, birthdays, weddings, retirement parties, baby showers, and more!

Materials:

- Celebrate cut file (or make one of your own!)
- Measuring tape
- Paper napkins
- Glitter iron-on
- Regular grip cutting mat
- Fine-tip blade
- Weeding tools
- Cricut EasyPress or iron
- EasyPress Mat or a towel to protect your work surface
- Optional: Iron-on protective sheet

Directions:

Step 1: Log into Cricut Design Space and upload the "Celebrate" cut file following the Cut File Upload instructions on page 28 of this book.

Step 2: Measure your napkin and where you want the design to be. Size your design by clicking on the design and using either the arrow that appears in the bottom right-hand corner of the design or the **Size** tool in the top toolbar. Click **Duplicate** to copy the image for the number of napkins you would like to decorate.

Step 2.

Step 3: Click **Make It**. Click the mirror slider under the cutting mat on the left-hand side of the screen. Set your cutting material to the type of HTV you're using and follow the prompts on the screen. Lay your iron-on with the color side down on the cutting mat then load your cutting mat into the machine using the arrow on the right-hand side of your Cricut. Once your mat is loaded, look for the Cricut C to start flashing, press the button, and your machine will start cutting. When your machine finishes cutting, press the arrow again and your mat will unload.

Step 3.

Step 3.

Step 4: Weed your iron-on, removing the iron-on around your design, leaving just the design on the clear plastic backing.

Step 4.

Step 5: Follow the instructions for applying the type of iron-on you're using to paper/cardstock. Iron your design onto each napkin. Once the plastic is cool enough to touch, peel away the plastic, leaving your design on the napkin.

Step 5.

Enjoy your beautiful napkins at your next big celebration!

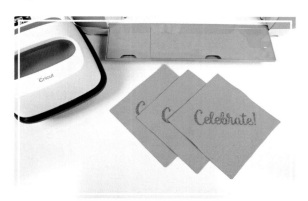

"Heading Straight to Dreamland" Pillowcase

Cricut Explore **or** Cricut Maker Project

Everywhere I go, I'm always on the lookout for new and interesting blank canvases to Cricut on. Pillowcases make a big, beautiful, blank canvas, and there are so many ways that you can customize them—names, quotes, sayings, initials, and favorite animals or characters are just a few ideas! I love how this pillowcase turned out with the combination of a beautiful script font, paired with an all-caps san serif font. I even used a flocked HTV for the heart so it's nice and fuzzy! Wash these pillowcases inside-out on delicate to get the most life out of them.

Materials:

- "Heading Straight to Dreamland" cut file
- Measuring tape
- Blank pillowcase
- HTV in your favorite colors
- Regular grip cutting mat (depending on the size of your design, you may need a 12 x 24-inch cutting mat)
- Fine-tip blade
- Weeding tools
- Cricut EasyPress or Iron
- EasyPress Mat or a towel to protect your work surface
- Optional: Brayer and iron-on protective sheet

Directions:

Step 1: Log into Cricut Design Space and upload the "Heading Straight to Dreamland" cut file following the Cut File Upload instructions on page 28 of this book. Click on each piece of the cut file and change it to the color of HTV that you will be using.

Step 1.

Step 2: Measure where you want the design to be on your pillowcase. Size your design by clicking on it and using either the arrow that appears in the bottom right-hand corner of the design or the Size tool in the top toolbar.

Step 2.

Step 3: Click Make It. Click the mirror slider under the cutting mat on the left-hand side of the screen. Set your cutting material to the type of HTV you're using and follow the prompts on the screen. Lay your iron-on with the color side down on the cutting mat then load your cutting mat into the machine using the arrow on the right-hand side of your Cricut. Once your mat is loaded, look for the Cricut C to start flashing, press the button, and your machine will start cutting. When your machine finishes cutting, press the arrow again and your mat will unload. Repeat with each color of HTV.

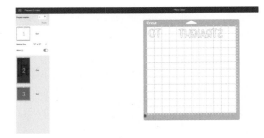

Step 3.

Step 3.

Step 4: Weed your HTV, removing the material around your design, leaving just the design on the clear plastic backing.

Step 4.

Step 5: Follow the instructions for applying the type of iron-on you're using to the material that your pillowcase is made from.

Step 5.

Optional: Use the iron-on protective sheet to give an extra layer of protection to your design. I also love to use the brayer tool with HTV to really push the vinyl into the fibers of the pillowcase between each press.

Step 6: Remove the clear plastic liner, revealing your design beneath.

Step 6.

Rest your head on your new pillowcase and drift off to dreamland!

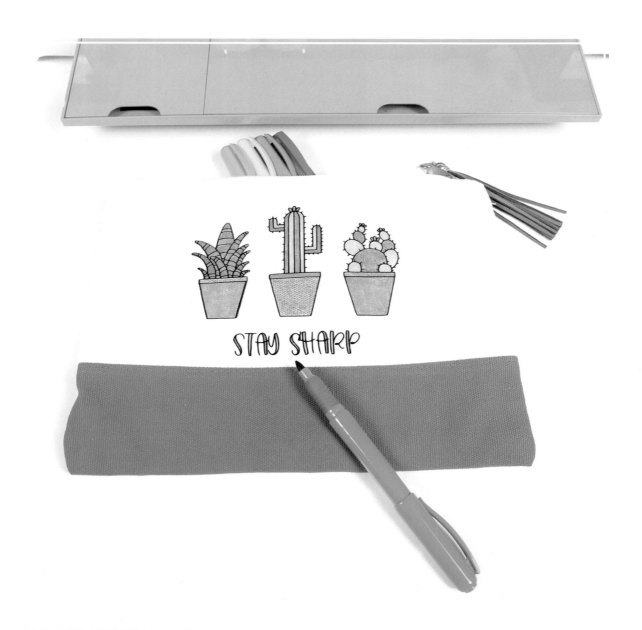

"Stay Sharp" Cactus Coloring Zippered Pouch

Cricut Explore **or** Cricut Maker Project (Cricut Joy Compatible)

Do you love to color? A few years ago, adult coloring books became all the rage and tweens, teens, and adults were reminded why kids love to color so much! It's so much fun and relaxing! This project takes coloring to a whole new level! We're using a fabric zippered pouch as our coloring canvas, using black HTV to create our picture, and then we're coloring it in using fabric markers. This project is easy to make and fun for all ages! I'm giving you the cut file for making a "Stay Sharp" cactus zippered pouch, but see where your creativity takes you. What else could you use for a coloring canvas? Tote bags, T-shirts, sweatshirts, pillowcases, baseball hats, and more! There are so many possibilities! I love giving these as gifts to kids with a handmade gift tag that says "Color Me" and a set of fabric markers.

Materials:

- "Stay Sharp" Cactus cut file
- Measuring tape
- Zippered fabric pouch
- Black HTV
- Regular grip cutting mat
- Fine-tip blade
- Weeding tools
- Cricut EasyPress or iron
- EasyPress Mat or a towel to protect your work surface
- Fabric markers
- Optional: Brayer and iron-on protective sheet

Directions:

Step 1: Log into Cricut Design Space and upload the "Stay Sharp" cactus cut file following the Cut File Upload instructions on page 28 of this book.

Step 2: Measure where you want the design to be on your zippered pouch. Size your design by clicking on it and using either the arrow that appears in the bottom right-hand corner of the design or the Size tool in the top toolbar.

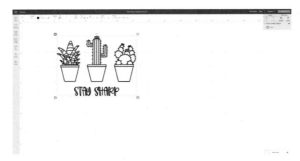

Step 2.

Step 3: Click Make It. Click the mirror slider under the cutting mat on the left-hand side of the screen. Set your cutting material to the type of HTV you're using and follow the prompts on the screen. Lay your iron-on with the color side down on the cutting mat, then load your cutting mat into the machine using the arrow on the right-hand side of your Cricut. Once your mat is loaded, look for the Cricut C to start flashing, press the button, and your machine will start cutting. When your machine finishes cutting, press the arrow again and your mat will unload.

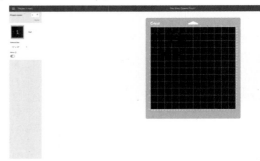

Step 3.

Step 3.

Step 4: Weed your HTV, removing the material around your design, leaving just the design on the clear plastic backing.

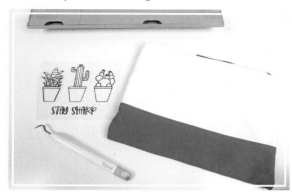

Step 4.

Step 5: Follow the instructions for applying the type of iron-on you're using to the material that your zippered pouch is made from.

Step 5.

Optional: Use the iron-on protective sheet to give an extra layer of protection to your design. I also love to use the brayer tool with HTV to really push the vinyl into the fibers of the bag between each press.

Step 6: Remove the clear plastic liner, revealing your design beneath. Color in your zippered pouch. I suggest putting a piece of cardstock inside the zippered pouch while coloring so that the ink doesn't bleed through to the other side of the zippered pouch.

Step 6.

Fill your adorable zippered pouch with all your favorite things like pens in your favorite colors, washi tape, lip balm, and more!

"The Kitchen is the Heart of the Home" Chalkboard Sign

Cricut Explore **or** Cricut Maker Project

I love using HTV on fabric, but there are other applications, as well! So far in this book, we've put HTV on a shirt, a pillowcase, a canvas bag, and paper napkins, so let's try it on wood! When you think of creating a wood sign using your Cricut, your first thought might be to use vinyl. Vinyl is a great choice for a wood sign, but if you're putting the sign in an area that might see moisture (like a kitchen or a bathroom), you might want to consider using iron-on. Where vinyl really loves smooth surfaces, iron-on loves sticking to texture (like the fibers of a shirt, or the roughness of wood). The iron-on will permanently adhere to the wood, and if you're putting it in your kitchen, you don't need to worry about moisture or steam causing the design to peel. I used a wood chalkboard sign I found in the wedding section of my local craft store. I think it would also look very cute for a weekly menu board. Put on your crafting caps! What area of your home will you make a wood sign for next? Prefer to use vinyl for this project? Go for it! Don't mirror your image and use transfer tape to transfer the design to your wood.

Materials:
- "The Kitchen is the Heart of the Home" cut file
- Measuring tape
- Wood sign
- White HTV
- Red HTV
- Regular grip cutting mat
- Fine-tip blade
- Weeding tools
- Cricut EasyPress or iron
- EasyPress Mat or a towel to protect your work surface
- Optional: Brayer and iron-on protective sheet

Directions:

Step 1: Log into Cricut Design Space and upload the "Kitchen is the Heart of the Home" cut file following the Cut File Upload instructions on page 28 of this book.

Step 2: Measure where you want the design to be on your wood sign. Size your design by clicking on it and using either the arrow that appears in the bottom right-hand corner of the design or the **Size** tool in the top toolbar.

Once your design is sized, click the **Ungroup** button in the right-hand toolbar. Next, select all the word pieces by pressing Shift on your keyboard and clicking on each piece in the right-hand toolbar. Then click **Attach**. This will make all the words cut in the places grouped together instead of in individual pieces.

Step 2.

Step 2.

Step 3: Click Make It. Click the mirror slider under the cutting mat on the left-hand side of the screen. Set your cutting material to the type of HTV you're using and follow the prompts on the screen. Lay your iron-on with the color side down on the cutting mat then load your cutting mat into the machine using the arrow on the right-hand side of your Cricut. Once your mat is loaded, look for the Cricut C to start flashing, press the button, and your machine will start cutting. When your machine finishes cutting, press the arrow again and your mat will unload. Repeat with each color of HTV.

Step 3.

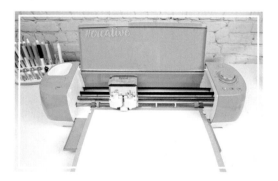

Step 3.

Step 4: Weed your HTV, removing the material around your design, leaving just the design on the clear plastic backing.

Step 5: Follow the instructions for applying the type of iron-on you are using to wood.

Step 5.

Optional: Use the iron-on protective sheet to give an extra layer of protection to your design. I also love to use the brayer tool with HTV to really push the vinyl into the fibers of the wood between each press.

Step 6: Peel away the plastic liner, revealing your design beneath.

There you have it! This gorgeous kitchen sign would make a great housewarming present or a handmade gift for someone who loves to cook or bake!

An Introduction to Fabric Projects

Let's Talk Fabric!

I was lucky enough to be one of the people invited to the top-secret launch of the Cricut Maker in August 2017. I was super excited about a bunch of the features of the new machine, but nothing had me more excited than the rotary blade. I love to sew, but I've never been particularly good at cutting fabric. I don't know what it is, but I have the hardest time using scissors or a manual rotary cutter to get precise cuts. Sewing is so much easier, and you get much better results, when you have perfectly cut fabric where all of your pieces perfectly align. Not only does the Cricut Maker cut fabric with the rotary blade, but it also cuts it fast! My Cricut Maker has saved me countless hours of fabric cutting and lets me focus on the part that I really enjoy—sewing!

The Cricut Maker can cut just about every fabric that you throw at it. Find the complete list at the back of this book (page 281).

Some of my favorite fabrics to cut with the Cricut Maker are:

- Quilting Cotton
- Felt
- Canvas
- Fleece
- Minky
- Flannel
- Denim
- Sequined Fabric
- Oilcloth

Pro-Crafter Tip
Invest in a 12 x 24-inch fabric cutting mat. You can still cut smaller projects on it that you would normally cut on a 12 x 12-inch cutting mat, but it also gives you the ability to cut larger projects!

Fabric Lingo

I love buying fabric collections in smaller cuts. It makes it easy to coordinate fabric for projects and gives you just enough fabric, without a ton leftover. Smaller cuts also fit really well on Cricut cutting mats without having to trim down too much (if at all). Cricut sells a limited range of fabric, precut in sizes to fit your mat, but there are also bundles marketed toward quilters available online and at fabric shops. Collections of different sizes of fabric bundled together have some fun names. Here are the terms for each size cut:

Fat Quarters: A collection from a fabric line where the fabric is cut in quarter-yard cuts, so each piece is approximately 18 inches by 21 inches.

Half-Yard Bundles: A collection from a fabric line where the fabric is cut in half-yard cuts, so each piece is approximately 18 inches by 44 inches.

Fat Eighth Bundles: A collection from a fabric line where fabric is cut in one-eighth of a yard cuts, so each piece is approximately 9 inches by 21 inches. This size works very nicely with the 12 x 24-inch Cricut FabricGrip Cutting Mat without having to be trimmed.

Layer Cakes: This is one of my favorite sizes for cutting with the Cricut. Each piece from the collection is cut 10 inches by 10 inches.

Jolly Bars: Each piece of fabric from the collection is cut 5 inches by 10 inches.

Charm Packs: Each piece of fabric from the collection is cut 5 inches by 5 inches.

Other Useful Tools & Materials for Working with Fabric

- **FabricGrip cutting mat:** A FabricGrip cutting mat has the perfect grip for keeping your fabric secure while cutting.
- **Rotary blade:** The perfect blade for cutting fabric when using your Cricut Maker. This blade is circular like a manual rotary cutter but can swivel 360 degrees for precise cuts.
- **Brayer tool:** Roll your brayer tool over your fabric once you've placed it on your cutting mat to really push the fibers of the fabric into the mat. This helps avoid your fabric slipping on the mat while it's being cut.
- **Manual rotary cutter, self-healing mat, and clear acrylic ruler:** The Cricut Maker makes cutting fabric so much easier, but you will still need to cut your fabric down to cutting-mat size. A manual rotary cutter, self-healing mat, and clear acrylic ruler makes this process a lot faster and easier.
- **Pins or Wonder Clips:** You'll use these for attaching cut fabric pieces together before sewing. I love how easy wonder clips are to use along the outside edges of fabric.
- **Fabric Scissors:** Every seamstress needs a pair!
- **Iron or EasyPress:** Now that I own an EasyPress, I'll often use this in place of an iron. Whichever you use, you'll need one to press your seams and make sure your fabric is nice and pressed.
- **Sewing Machine:** Because it's so much easier than sewing by hand!

Sloth Sleep Mask

Cricut Maker Project

What is it about sloths that make them just so darn cute? I'm seriously in love with these slow-moving little critters. My kiddos are in love with sloths, too, and are constantly coming to me with sloth facts. ("Mom, did you know that the number one cause of death among sloths happens when they are going to the bathroom? They come down out of the tree to go poop and they move so slowly when they're down there that their predators get them!") Yes, we are a family of sloth lovers. I also have quite an affinity for sleep masks—I love making them in fun animal shapes and think they are just as cute as can be! This sweet little sleep mask makes an adorable handmade gift and is perfect for wearing to slumber parties. Make a whole family of sleepy sloth sleep masks and give them to everyone you love!

Materials:

- Sloth Sleep Mask cut file
- FabricGrip adhesive cutting mat
- Regular grip cutting mat
- Cricut Rotary Blade
- Fine-tip blade
- Heat transfer vinyl (I used brown, black, and white for this project.)
- 10 x 12-inch piece of fabric for the front of your mask (I used quilting cotton)
- 10 x 12-inch piece of fabric for the back of the mask (I used fleece)
- 12-inch piece of black elastic
- Cricut Iron-On Protective Sheet
- Cricut EasyPress or iron
- Sewing machine
- Thread in coordinating colors
- Scissors
- Wonder clips or pins
- Sewing needle

Directions:

Step 1: Log into Cricut Design Space and upload the Sloth Sleep Mask cut files following the Cut File Upload instructions on page 28 of this book.

Step 2: Size your design so that it's 8.5 inches wide by clicking on the design and using either the arrow that appears in the bottom right-hand corner of the design or the Size tool in the top toolbar.

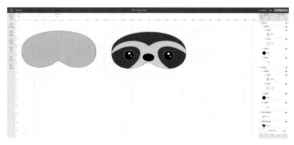

Step 2.

Step 3: Click Make It. Follow the prompts to cut each piece of the sleep mask, loading the appropriate material and cutting blade. The sleep mask–shaped pieces will be cut out of fabric using the FabricGrip adhesive cutting mat and the rotary blade.

The sloth face pieces will be cut out of HTV (make sure you load your HTV with the shiny colored side down) using the regular grip cutting mat and fine-tip blade.

Load your cutting mat with each material, select the appropriate material from the drop-down menu, and then load the cutting mat into the machine using the arrow on the right-hand side of your Cricut. Once your mat is loaded, look for the Cricut C to start flashing, press the button, and your machine will start cutting. When your machine finishes cutting, press the arrow again and your mat will unload. Repeat for each material you are cutting.

Step 3.

Step 4: After you've cut all your pieces, it's time to apply the iron-on shapes to the front of your sleep mask fabric. This involves layering, which can be tricky because you don't want to scorch your iron-on. I find that the Cricut Iron-On Protective Sheet makes layering so much easier. Check the EasyPress Heat Setting Guide for the type of HTV you're using to know what temperature and for how long each piece gets pressed.

Apply the sloth's hairline and eye patches first, followed by the whites of the eyes, the black parts of the eyes, the white dots in the eyes, and the nose.

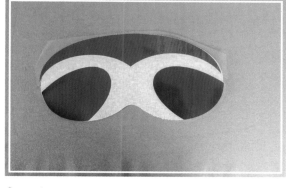

Step 4.

Step 4.

Step 4.

Pro-Crafter Tip

Layering HTV can be tricky. I suggest pressing your first layer for 5 to 10 seconds or until it *just* adheres to the fabric, allowing you to remove the clear plastic liner. Repeat for each layer, pressing for just 5 to 10 seconds or until the HTV sticks to the layer below. Use an iron-on protective sheet to help protect your HTV and keep it from scorching.

Step 5: Now it's time to sew! Pin your elastic onto the back fleece part of the sleep mask. Let the elastic overhang the edge of the mask by ½ inch on each side.

Next, you want to make a "sleep mask sandwich." The side of the fleece with the elastic pinned to it should be facing up. On top of that, lay the front of your face mask with eyes and nose facing down. Since the face of the mask has iron-on applied to it, I suggest using wonder clips so you don't poke holes in your iron-on and/or being strategic with where you place your pins.

Step 5.

Step 6: Sew all the way around the outside of your sleep mask using a ¼-inch seam allowance and making sure to leave a 1-inch or bigger gap to flip your mask right-side out.

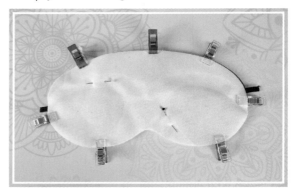

Step 6.

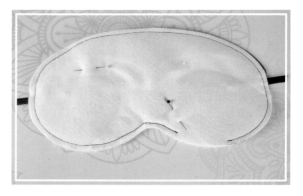

Step 7: Flip your mask right-side out, press into place (make sure you use the iron-on protective sheet if pressing the sloth's face), and sew closed the opening you used to turn the sloth mask right-side out using needle and thread.

And there you have it! An adorable Sloth Sleep Mask! Wear it for a guaranteed sleepy sloth sleep!

Over-the-Collar Pet Bandana

Cricut Maker Project

I'm the "dog mother" of two adorable, scruffy rescue pups named Mochi (age 5) and Marley (age 1). My family also works with a local rescue group as a foster home for dogs while they wait to find their fur-ever families. One of my favorite things about taking my dogs to the groomer (besides the fact that they come back looking and smelling great) is that our groomer always puts a cute little bandana on them. There's something about a pet in a bandana that's just so darn cute! The bandanas our groomer sends our dogs home wearing are just pieces of fabric with raw edges. They end up fraying quickly. So I decided to create my own version that has durability! These over-the-collar pet bandanas slip over your pet's collar so you don't have to worry about tying them around your pet's neck. They are great for dogs or cats, and thanks to Cricut Design Space, you can make them for any size pet! These make great gifts for pet owners, or for pets themselves. Make them in a ton of fun patterns and colors and turn your furry friend into a fashionista!

Materials:

- Over-the-Collar Pet Bandana cut file
- Measuring tape
- FabricGrip adhesive cutting mat
- Fabric (You can use one pattern of fabric or two different patterns and have your bandana be reversible.)
- Cricut Rotary Blade
- Cricut EasyPress or iron
- Sewing machine
- Thread in coordinating colors
- Scissors
- Wonder clips or pins

Directions:

Step 1: Log into Cricut Design Space and upload the Pet Bandana cut file following the PNG Upload instructions on page 23 of this book.

Step 2: Measure your pet's collar and where you would like the bandana to lay on the collar. Click on the cut file and size the area at the base of the triangle (the area between the two arrows in the photo) to that size. Click the Duplicate button to make a second piece that is the same size.

Step 3: Click Make It. Follow the prompts to choose the type of fabric you're using. Lay the fabric onto the FabricGrip mat. Load your cutting mat into the machine using the arrow button on your Cricut Maker and then press the flashing Cricut C. Repeat with your second piece of fabric.

Step 3.

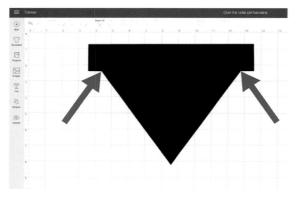
Step 2.

Step 3.

Step 4: Remove your cut fabric from the cutting mat. Next, we want to fold over the edges of the tabs so that we don't have exposed fabric edges when we slide the bandana over the collar. Fold the tab over on top so that the edge lines up with the base of the triangle. Fold once more so that you have a nice, neat hem and press into place using your EasyPress or iron. Repeat with tab 1 and 2 on both pieces of fabric.

Step 4.

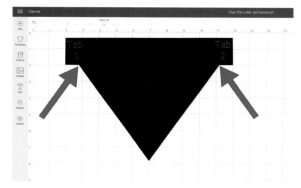

Step 4.

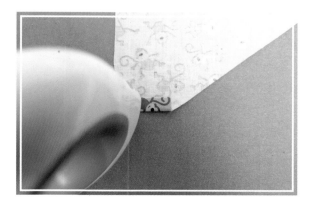

Step 4.

Step 5: Stitch down each hem using a ⅛-inch seam allowance.

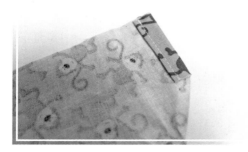

Step 5.

Step 6: Next, line up the edges of both pieces of your bandana with the printed side of the fabric sandwiched in the middle. Stitch across the top edge of the bandana using a ¼-inch seam allowance. Next, stitch from the base of your hemmed tab, down to the bottom of the triangle, and back up to the base of the second hemmed tab. Make sure to leave the hemmed tabs open; this is how you'll flip your bandana right-side out and where you will feed the collar through.

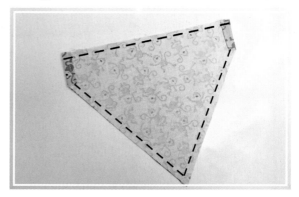

Step 6.

Step 7: Flip your bandana right-side out, making sure to push out all your corners. Iron your bandana so the edges are nice and crisp.

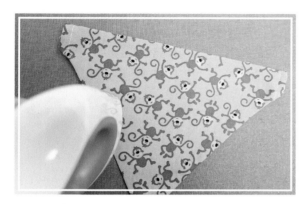

Step 7.

You now have an adorable over-the-collar pet bandana! Feed your pet's collar through the bandana and put it on your pet. This is such a cute way to let your pet's personality really shine!

Finished project.

"Adventure Awaits" Travel Pillow

I love a good vacation! For my family, sometimes that means climbing on an airplane and jetting off somewhere fun, but it also means climbing in our family minivan and going for a good, old-fashioned road trip. There's nothing like the rumble of an engine to put a child to sleep; my kids fall asleep in the car or on a plane all the time. I always cringe when I see their little heads lolling around in their sleep, so I decided to pull out my Cricut Maker and my sewing machine and do something about it—I made them travel pillows! One of the very best things about having a Cricut is being able to customize things, so in addition to showing you how to make a travel pillow, I'm also sharing a cut file for a super cute Adventure Awaits iron-on design. Once you've got the basics down for making a travel pillow, use your imagination and create different adorable iron-on designs for each travel pillow you make! Maybe a sloth travel pillow to go with your Sloth Sleep Mask from page 125 of this book? Head on over to **HelloCreativeFamily.com** and search "sloth travel" for an adorable free cut file that's perfect for a sloth travel pillow!

Materials:

- Travel Pillow cut file
- 12 x 24-inch FabricGrip adhesive cutting mat
- Regular grip cutting mat
- Cricut Rotary Blade
- Fine-tip blade
- Iron-on Vinyl (I used gold glitter for this project)
- 2 (12 x 24–inch) pieces of fabric (I used a solid-colored fabric for the front piece and a patterned piece for the back)
- Cricut EasyPress or iron
- Sewing machine
- Thread in coordinating colors
- Scissors
- Wonder clips or pins
- Batting
- Sewing needle

Directions:

Step 1: Log into Cricut Design Space and upload the travel pillow cut files following the Cut File Upload instructions on page 28 of this book.

Step 2: Size the cut file so the pillow shape is 11.5 inches tall. Do this by clicking on the image and either using the arrow button in the bottom right-hand corner or the **Size** tool in the top toolbar. Click the **Duplicate** button to make a copy of the pillow shape so that you have two of them to cut.

Step 2.

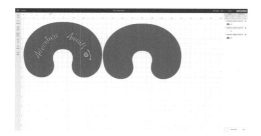

Step 2.

Step 3: Click **Make It**. Click the mirror slider on the "Adventure Awaits" cutting mat. Follow the prompts on the screen. Cut the "Adventure Awaits" out of HTV using a fine-tip blade and a regular grip cutting mat. Place the HTV with the shiny color side facing down on the mat. Cut the fabric using the rotary blade on a 12 x 24-inch fabric cutting mat.

Step 3.

Step 3.

Step 4: Remove the fabric and iron-on from the cutting mats. Weed your vinyl, removing the area around your design from the clear plastic sheet, leaving your design behind. Don't forget the pieces inside your letters. Heat your EasyPress or iron using the heat settings for the type of iron-on that you're using from the EasyPress temperature guide. Apply your iron-on following the instructions for the type of iron-on you're using. Remove the clear plastic liner, revealing your design beneath.

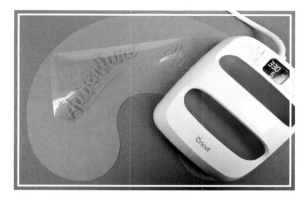

Step 4.

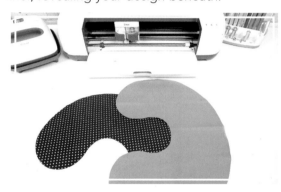

Step 4.

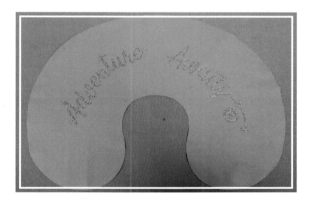

Step 4.

Step 4.

Step 5: Now it's time to sew your travel pillow. Lay the two pieces of your travel pillow so that all the edges are lined up and the printed part of the fabric is facing the center of your fabric sandwich. Pin in place.

Sew all the way around your travel pillow using a ¼-inch seam allowance. Make sure you leave a 2 to 4-inch section open so you can flip your sleep pillow right-side out and stuff it.

Step 6: Flip your travel pillow right-side out. Use batting to stuff the pillow, making sure to really pack it in and get batting in all the curves. Once you're satisfied with how full your pillow is stuffed, use a needle and thread to sew up the open section.

Step 6.

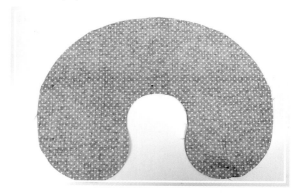

Step 5.

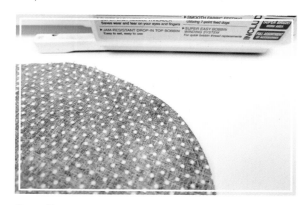

Step 5.

Step 6.

Now you have a gorgeous travel pillow for your next big vacation! Make sure you visit HelloCreativeFamily.com for other Cricut Maker travel ideas like our 30 Minute Passport Holder and 20-Minute Makeup Bag!

DIY RAG QUILT

Cricut Maker Project

When my son was six months old, I made him a DIY rag quilt for his first Christmas present. I made it with the intention of making a second one for my daughter that I would give to her the following year for Christmas. It ended up taking me six years, and the invention of the Cricut Maker, to get around to it. Here's the truth: I really enjoyed sewing the blanket for my son, but I hated cutting all of that fabric! For rag quilts, you need to cut squares for the front of the quilt, squares for the back of the quilt, and squares of batting for the center! That's a lot of precision cutting—but guess what? With the Cricut Maker and the rotary blade, you can have your cutting machine do the hard work for you and you just get to do the fun part—the sewing! This pretty quilt makes a great gift for a new baby or anyone who you want to wrap in a bit of love!

Note: So, what is a rag quilt? A rag quilt is a quilt that has exposed seams (instead of the seams being hidden inside). The seams fray once washed, giving it a unique look with each block framed by the seams. Each of the exposed seams is snipped multiple times with scissors to encourage fraying, but this also makes the quilt fairly forgiving of little mistakes. You can make your rag quilt out of a variety of fabrics including, but not limited to, quilting cotton, minky, and flannel.

Materials listed on page 144.

Materials:

- Paper and pencil
- Self-Healing Mat, rotary cutter, and acrylic ruler
- Fabric and batting*
- 12 x 24-inch FabricGrip adhesive cutting mat
- Cricut Rotary Blade
- Spray adhesive (optional)
- Cricut EasyPress or iron
- Sewing machine
- Thread in coordinating colors
- Fabric scissors
- Wonder clips or pins

*My quilt was 5 blocks by 7 blocks in size. I used 35 (10 x 10-inch) blocks of fabric from Riley Blake's Hello Baby fabric line for the front, 35 (10 x 10-inch) blocks of pink minky for the back, and 35 (8 x 8-inch) blocks of Warm & Natural Cotton Batting for the interior.

Note: You can make this project as big or as small as you would like it to be. You can use small squares or big, giant squares. You can have 12 squares in your quilt, or 200 squares in your quilt—it's completely up to you! I'm going to teach you how to make the quilt in any size you want so that you can customize it any way you want, anytime you want to! Each quilt square will have 2 inches ragged from it, which is important to keep in mind when calculating the size of your finished quilt, so a 10 by 10-inch square will become a 8 by 8-inch square once your quilt is assembled.

Directions:

Step 1: Visualize your quilt! Maybe you want a lap quilt for snuggling on the couch. Perhaps you want it to cover your niece at night on her twin-sized bed. Or you could plan on giving a king-sized quilt as a wedding gift. Take out that pencil and paper and figure out what size you want your quilt to be and then how many blocks you want in each row. For my quilt, I had seven rows of quilt blocks with five (10 x 10-inch) blocks in each row.

Step 2: Log into Cricut Design Space and create a new project. Select a square from under the Shapes button. Size the square to the size that you want your quilt squares. Next, click the Duplicate button to create how many squares you want for the front of your quilt. So, if you want the front of your quilt to have 35 squares, duplicate it until you have 35 squares.

Now, let's do the back of your quilt. Create a new square in a different color from the front of your quilt. Size it to the same size as the squares for the front of your quilt and duplicate it so that you have the correct number of squares for the back of your quilt.

Finally, we're going to do the squares for the batting. You want to have a 1-inch border of fabric all the way around your batting so you can rag your quilt without the batting showing. Deduct 2 inches from the size of your main quilt blocks to get the size for your batting. So, if your quilt blocks are 10 inches, your batting should be 8 inches. If your quilt blocks are 6 inches, your quilt batting should be 4 inches. Duplicate the square until you have the same number of squares as you have for the front of your quilt. So, in my case, 35.

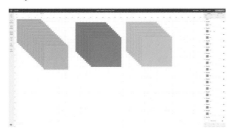

Step 2.

Step 3: Using your self-healing mat, rotary cutter, and acyrlic ruler, cut your fabric and batting into long strips that are slightly wider in width than how large you will be cutting them. For example, I cut my batting so that it was 9 inches wide (my Cricut Maker cut the finished batting blocks so that they were 8 x 8 inches) and minky so that it was 11 inches wide (my Cricut maker cut the finished minky blocks so that they were 10 x 10 inches).

Step 3.

Step 4: Click Make It. Select your Cricut Maker and then select the type of fabric you're cutting. Load your cutting mat with fabric, put your rotary cutter into your Cricut Maker, load your mats into your machine, and start cutting!

I used long strips of fabric and let the excess fabric fall off the end of my cutting mat. Once the blocks on the mat were cut, I moved my fabric up on the mat and reloaded it into the Maker to cut the next blocks.

Step 4.

Step 5: Now that you have your fabric cut, it's time to get sewing! The first step is to assemble each of your quilt blocks. To do this, you want to stack a square of your backing (in my case, the minky), a square of your batting (this should be centered in the middle with a 1-inch border all the way around), and then a layer of your top fabric (in my case, the quilter's cotton). I sprayed fabric spray adhesive inside each of my quilt block sandwiches to keep them from sliding around while I was sewing.

Next, you want to sew an X on each quilt block. Start in one corner and sew a straight line down and across the block to the opposite corner. Repeat on the opposite side. Do this to all your quilt block sandwiches.

Once I have all of the quilt block sandwiches sewn together, I like to lay my quilt out to see how I want to assemble it. When I have the layout I like, I put each row into a stack and number it with which row it is.

Step 5.

Step 5.

Step 6: Next, you're going to sew together your quilt blocks to create each row of your quilt. To do this, take the first two squares from your first row stack. Stack them together so the fabric you want on the front of your blanket is facing out and the minky backing is facing in. Sew down the edge where you want your two quilt blocks to join together using a 1-inch seam allowance.

Repeat this process, adding on each quilt block for that row until you have finished your first row of your quilt. Set that row aside and repeat for each row of your quilt.

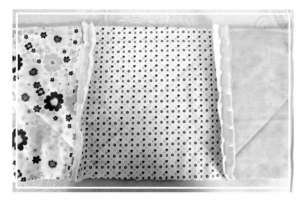

Step 6.

Step 7: Next, you want to join your rows together. Take your first two rows of your quilt and lay them one on top of the other with the fabric you want for the front of your blanket facing out and the backing facing in. Line up each seam, nesting them together, and then wonder clip or pin into place.

Sew down the edge joining the row together using a 1-inch seam allowance. Repeat with each row of your quilt.

Step 7.

Step 7.

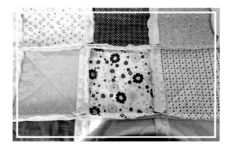

Step 7.

Step 8: Finish the edges of your blanket. Now that your quilt blocks are all sewn together, you want to finish the edges. Using a 1-inch seam allowance, sew all the way around the four sides of your blanket, using either a straight stitch or a zig zag stitch.

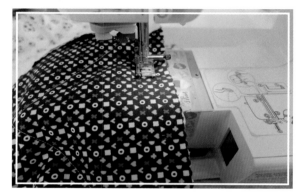

Step 8.

Step 9: Rag your quilt. Grab your scissors and cut snips every ¼ to ½ inch all the way around the outside edge of your blanket, as well as on each of the exposed seams. You will want to cut through the quilting cotton as well as the minky—but pay careful attention that you only cut the fabric and don't accidentally snip the stitches!

Step 9.

Step 10: Wash your quilt to help encourage the fray. After I do all my snips, I always throw my rag quilt into the washer and dryer. This helps to get the fraying going on all of the seams and makes it extra soft and snuggly!

And there you have it! You're all done! You have a beautiful rag quilt that you made all by yourself, without the headache of precision-cutting fabric by hand! My daughter loves hers, and with the minky backing, it's so soft and snuggly.

5-MINUTE TISSUE HOLDER

Cricut Maker Project

This might just be the most practical project in this whole entire book. I dare you to find a person who couldn't use a tissue holder for their purse, backpack, or jacket pocket! If you have a nose, you can use one of these awesome little tissue holders. I love giving tissue holders as stocking stuffers for Christmas. I have so much fun finding the perfect fabric for each person to make it one-of-a-kind. This is also a wonderful fabric scrap project. The best thing about these tissue holders, though, is that once you've gotten the hang of making them, they only take 5 minutes to make! Yep, you read that right—5 minutes!!! Ready to make one? Let's get started!

Materials:

- Enough fabric to cut 5 (4.5 x 6.5-inch) rectangles
- 12 x 24-inch FabricGrip adhesive cutting mat
- Cricut Rotary Blade
- EasyPress or iron
- Sewing machine
- Thread in coordinating colors
- Fabric scissors
- Pins or wonder clips
- Travel-sized tissue packet

Directions:

Step 1: Log into Cricut Design Space and create a new project. Select a square from under the **Shapes** button. Click on the square and then click the **Lock** button in the bottom left-hand corner to unlock the size proportions. Change the size of your square to 4.5 inches by 6.5 inches in the sizing box in the upper toolbox. You now have a rectangle. Click the **Duplicate** button to copy your rectangle four times so that you have 5 rectangles in total.

Step 1.

Step 2: Click **Make It**. Select your Cricut Maker and then select the type of fabric you're cutting. Load your cutting mat with fabric, put your rotary cutter into your Cricut Maker, load your mats into your machine, and start cutting!

Step 2.

Step 3: Carefully remove your fabric from your cutting mat. Fold and press with your iron two of your pieces of fabric lengthwise (print facing out), two of your pieces of fabric widthwise (print facing out), and leave your fifth piece flat.

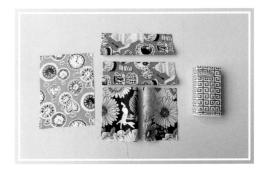

Step 3.

Step 4: Lay the piece of fabric that you left flat on the table with the print side facing up. Next, you will lay out the four top pieces of fabric. With each piece, you want the raw edge turned so it's lined up with the raw edge of the bottom piece of fabric. You want to lay them out almost the way you do when closing a box that you don't want to tape.

I lay them down in this order with the folded edge facing the center and the raw edge facing out:

1. Top long piece.
2. Right side short piece with the top edge overlapping the previous piece you laid down.
3. Bottom long piece with the right side overlapping the bottom of the previous piece you laid down.
4. Left side short piece with the bottom edge overlapping the previous piece you laid down and the top edge tucked underneath the top long piece.

The side that is currently facing up will be on the inside of your tissue holder when it's finished, so if you like the layout, flip the four pieces so they're facing down. If you're not picky about your fabric design layout, leave as is.

When you have all four pieces laid out on top of your bottom piece, make sure the edges are lined up and pin into place.

Step 4(1).

Step 4(2).

Step 4(3).

Step 4(4).

Step 4.

Step 5: Straight stitch around all four sides of your tissue holder, leaving a ½-inch seam allowance.

Step 5.

Optional: Zig-zag stitch around all four sides of your tissue holder, trying to line up the inside part of your zig-zag stitch as close to your straight stitch as possible.

Step 5 Optional.

Step 6: Trim away excess fabric and clip corners.

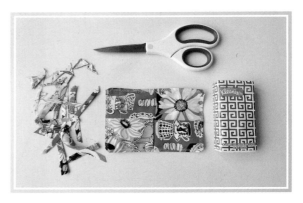

Step 6.

Step 7: Flip right-side out and put your travel-sized tissue packet inside.

Enjoy! These tissue holders make adorable gifts. They're perfect for school-aged children and college students to put in their backpacks, as well as in purses and jacket pockets. Plus, they make really cute handmade teacher gifts, as well!

An Introduction to Basswood, Balsa Wood, and Chipboard

Let's Talk Basswood, Balsa Wood, and Chipboard!

The Cricut Knife Blade opened the door to a whole new world of crafting possibilities—especially for home decor crafters! There are so many incredible things you can make by cutting chipboard, basswood, and balsa wood.

I'm not going to sugarcoat it: cutting basswood, balsa wood, and chipboard with your Cricut Maker takes time. There's a bit of a learning curve to it, and there will be times when your projects break when you're trying to take them off the mat, or when you get frustrated because your knife blade just doesn't cut all the way through. Yes, it can be a frustrating process, but when your project comes out just the way you dreamed it would, it's SO AMAZING! I'm sharing some knife blade success tips below, so before long, you will be an expert!

In the four projects in this chapter, I use basswood and chipboard because those are two products that Cricut produces and sells; however, you could interchange basswood, balsa wood, or chipboard for most of the home decor projects.

Most chipboard, balsa wood, and basswood on the market is brown. To add color, I like using paint, vinyl, printable vinyl, or even iron-on vinyl! I've shown projects using each of those techniques in the upcoming section.

The knife blade can only be used in the Cricut Maker, and there are a few "best practices" when using these materials that will give you the most success.

Cricut Maker Knife Blade Success Tips

- First things first—make sure you calibrate your knife blade after inserting it into the machine. This just takes a minute and uses a piece of paper. Definitely worth the time to get precision cutting. To do this, log into Cricut Design Space. In the upper left-hand corner, you'll see a square made of three lines. Click the square and a pop-up menu will appear with calibration listed. Click on Calibration and follow the prompts.
- Make sure you size your design so that no area is thinner than a pencil eraser. This will help avoid pieces breaking.
- Make sure you move all four of your white star wheels all the way to the right-hand side of your machine. The white star wheels can be found on the metal roller rod that your

mat goes under at the front of the machine. Push those bad boys all the way to the right.

- Make sure your cutting material is a maximum width of 11 inches.
- Position your chipboard, basswood, or balsa wood in the upper left-hand corner of your mat.
- Tape your cutting material to the mat using masking tape or painter's tape.
- Make sure you set aside time to complete your project. The knife blade works by making multiple cuts until it cuts all the way through the material. Depending on how big/complex your project is, it could possibly take hours for your machine to cut.
- Speaking of time, you probably won't want to set your machine and leave it. I highly suggest you make sure you check your work every few cuts/do not leave your machine unattended. When your machine starts cutting, on the Cricut Design Space screen it will say something like "3 out of 12 cuts completed, 20 minutes remain." If you are using a brand-new knife blade for your project, the knife blade can cut through much quicker than Design Space expects it to. You can check your work by using the Pause button on the Cricut Maker machine.
- Play around with cutting your design mirrored. Some crafters swear by cutting their materials with a knife blade mirrored and think that they get a cleaner cut on the part closest to the mat. Experiment with mirroring your image and see what you think!
- Since cutting with a knife blade takes so much longer than cutting with other blades, the last thing you would want to do is lose your connection to your machine! You may want to hook your computer directly to your Cricut Maker using a USB cable. Some of my crafty friends also suggest not running other programs on their computers while their knife blade is cutting.
- Have fun! There are so many incredible projects you could make with your Maker. The sky and your imagination is the limit!

Before you head to the craft store and stock up on materials, here are the thicknesses of each material the Cricut Knife Blade can cut:

- **Balsa wood:** $\frac{1}{16}$ inches (1.6mm) and $\frac{3}{32}$ inches (2.4mm)
- **Basswood:** $\frac{1}{16}$ inches (1.6mm) and $\frac{1}{32}$ inches (0.8mm)
- **Chipboard:** 0.37mm, 0.55mm, 1.5mm, and 2.0mm

Other Useful Tools & Materials for Working with Basswood, Balsa Wood, and Chipboard

- **Cricut Maker with a Cricut Knife Blade:** Unfortunately, this one isn't optional. The Cricut Maker with the Cricut Knife Blade is the only way you can cut basswood, balsa wood, and chipboard using a Cricut.
- **StrongGrip cutting mat:** It takes multiple passes and extra time to cut basswood, balsa wood, and chipboard. A StrongGrip mat will help make sure your cutting material stays adhered over multiple cuts.
- **Masking tape or painter's tape:** You will want this to hold your cutting material down on the mat. The last thing you want is your design to shift halfway through the cutting process.
- **Cricut True Control Knife and self-healing cutting mat:** There will be times when the majority of your design is cut all the way through, but there might be a tight corner where the knife blade didn't make its way all the way through. Using a Cricut True Control Knife and self-healing cutting mat is a great way to cut through those areas where the Cricut didn't quite get it done.

DIY Photo Puzzle

Cricut Maker Project

I love giving photo gifts. I think they're the ultimate personalized handmade gift. One of the things I was really excited about with the Cricut Maker was using the knife blade to cut chipboard and basswood. I remember thinking *How fun would it be to make a puzzle using my Cricut?* Then a few weeks later, I noticed several puzzle templates show up in the Cricut image library! It was like Cricut had read my mind. This project is easy to make, but because of the complexity of the design and cutting it out of chipboard, it will take your Cricut approximately an hour to cut, so make sure you factor in time if you're making this as a handmade gift. Pick your favorite photo and let the fun begin!

Materials:

- Your favorite photo
- Printable vinyl
- Printer
- LightGrip cutting mat
- Fine-point blade
- Cricut chipboard in either 1.5mm or 2mm
- StrongGrip cutting mat
- Masking or painter's tape
- Cricut knife blade
- Glue

Directions:

Note: *Make sure to read Cricut Maker Knife Blade Success Tips on page 157 of this book for best cutting results.*

Step 1: Upload a photo to Cricut Design Space by clicking the Upload button, selecting your file, choosing Complex Image, and then saving your file as a print-and-cut file.

Step 2: Click the Image button and search for "Puzzle." Select one of Cricut's puzzle cut files.

Step 2.

Step 3: Click on the puzzle design and click Ungroup from the right-hand toolbar. Lay the solid bottom part of the puzzle on top of your photo in Design Space (if your photo is in front of the bottom layer of the puzzle, right click and click Bring to Front or Send to Back). Position the bottom of your puzzle over the photo where you want the puzzle to be. Select both your photo and the bottom puzzle piece and click the Slice button. Your photo will now be cut the same size as your puzzle. Delete extra pieces.

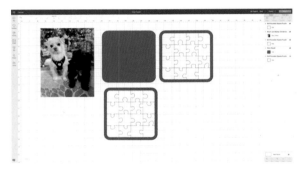

Step 3.

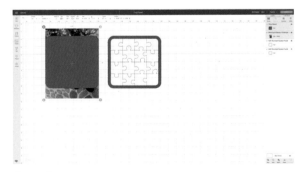

Step 3.

Step 4: Click Duplicate to copy the part of the puzzle that has the puzzle pieces. Place it over the top of your photo. Align the puzzle and the photos so that all edges line up. With the puzzle pieces and the photo both lined up and selected, click Attach.

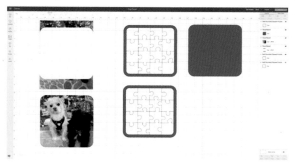

Step 4.

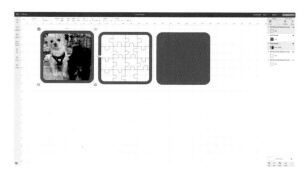

Step 4.

Step 5: Click Make It. You first will be prompted to print your photo. Do this on your sheet of printable vinyl. Then put the printed vinyl on a LightGrip cutting mat, load into your machine, and cut. Let your machine cut and then unload your mat.

Step 5.

Step 6: Now it's time to cut the chipboard. Slide the white star wheels of your cutting machine to the right-hand side of your machine. Place a piece of chipboard onto a StrongGrip cutting mat. Tape into place using masking tape or painter's tape. On the left-hand side of the screen, select your mats that will be cut out of the chipboard. Click the Edit button and move your cut so that it's 1 inch down and 1 inch to the right. Change your cutting material to chipboard. Put your knife blade into your Cricut and then load your cutting mat into the machine by pressing the arrow and then press the flashing Cricut C. Repeat step 6 with the second piece of chipboard for the second piece of your puzzle.

Note: As your machine cuts, you will see a status circle in Cricut Design Space telling you how many passes your knife blade has made on your design. I suggest pausing your machine (by pressing the Pause button on the right-hand side of the machine) every few cuts after you get to 10 cuts and checking to see if the knife blade has cut all the way through your chipboard yet. Often, the knife blade cuts through sooner than Design Space thinks it will. If your project is cut through, press the arrow to eject. If it hasn't cut through yet, press the Pause button again for the machine to continue cutting.

Always make sure to check if the design is cut through before ejecting the cutting mat. If your Cricut has gone through all the passes and the design still isn't cut out, you can press the Cricut C and it will begin cutting again in the exact same path. However, if you eject the cutting mat and reload it, you aren't guaranteed that your cuts will be on the exact same lines.

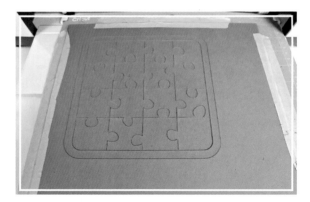

Step 6.

Step 6.

Step 7: Transfer your vinyl stickers to each piece of the puzzle. You will have the option of making the border out of your printed vinyl photo or you can alternatively paint the chipboard using your favorite color.

Step 8: Lay the bottom of your puzzle on a work-safe surface. Glue the border on top of the puzzle bottom. Allow to dry and then assemble your puzzle!

Step 8.

Step 7.

Photo puzzles make an excellent handmade gift. Put an old wedding photo on a puzzle for a fiftieth anniversary gift. Put a baby photo on a puzzle for a first birthday present. Put a class photo on a puzzle for a one-of-a-kind teacher gift! What will you put on your photo puzzle? Make sure you share a photo of your finished puzzle with me by using the hashtag #hcfcricutcrafts and tagging @hellocreativefamily on Instagram!

Step 7.

Llama Pencil Holder

One of the things that I think most artists have in common is that we have an over-abundance of supplies. I love my craft supplies, and besides my craft studio, my second favorite place is hanging out in the aisles of my local craft store. I have more pens, pencils, washi tape, paintbrushes, colored pencils, and markers than I'll ever be able to use. I love grouping them together and putting them in pretty jars, cups, and mugs. For this project, we're taking a mason jar and turning it into one of my very favorite animals—a llama! I cut this llama out of chipboard, but you could also use basswood or balsa wood if you prefer! Use your imagination to decorate your llama jar with pretty embellishments! Play around with the colors that you use for her tassels, make her a pretty flower crown, or even decorate the lip of the jar with brightly colored yarn!

Materials:

- Llama cut file
- Mason jar
- Ruler or measuring tape
- Cricut chipboard in either 1.5mm or 2mm
- StrongGrip cutting mat
- Masking or painter's tape
- Cricut Knife Blade
- Vinyl (I used black for the nose and eyes, white for the dots in the eyes, and pink and aqua for the tassels.)
- Foam paint brush
- Acrylic paint (I used white for the llama and aqua blue for the jar.)
- Weeding tools
- Transfer tape
- Brayer or scraper
- Glue gun and hot glue sticks
- Optional: Extra embellishments to decorate your llama (I used paper flowers)

Directions:

Note: *Make sure to read Cricut Maker Knife Blade Success Tips on page 157 of this book for best cutting results.*

Step 1: Log into Cricut Design Space and upload the Llama pencil holder cut file following the Cut File Upload instructions on page 28 of this book.

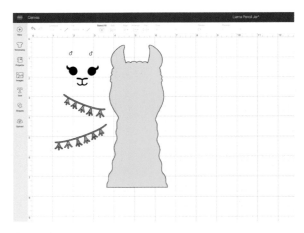

Step 1.

Step 2: Measure your mason jar to determine how large you would like your llama to be. I made mine 7 inches tall. Size your design by clicking on it and using either the arrow that appears in the bottom right hand corner of the design or the Size tool in the top toolbar.

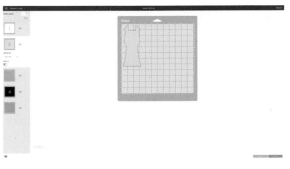

Step 2.

Step 3: Click Make It. I find that my chipboard cuts cleaner on the side closest to the mat, so I suggest mirroring each of the pieces by clicking the mirror slider on each mat on the left-hand side of the screen. Cut the llama body out of chipboard using a StrongGrip mat and knife blade. Use masking tape or painter's tape to tape your chipboard to the cutting mat.

Use a regular grip mat and your fine-tip blade for cutting the eyes, nose, mouth, and tassels out of vinyl.

Following the prompts on the screen, load your cutting mat into the machine using the arrow on the right-hand side of your Cricut. Once your mat is loaded, look for the Cricut C to start flashing, press the button, and your machine will start cutting. When your machine finishes cutting, press the arrow again and your mat will unload.

Step 3.

Step 4: Paint your chipboard llama and mason jar, allowing the paint to dry between each coat.

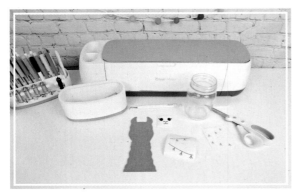

Step 4.

Step 5: Weed your vinyl, removing the area around each design and leaving just the design on the paper backing.

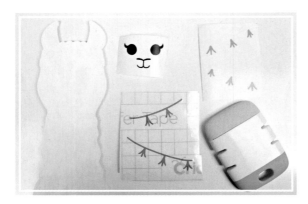

Step 5.

Step 6: Once the paint has dried on your llama, cut a piece of transfer tape a tiny bit bigger than your largest vinyl design. Peel the paper backing off the transfer tape and lay it so that the sticky part is lying on top of one of your vinyl designs. Rub your scraper or brayer tool overtop of the transfer tape, pushing the tape onto the vinyl. Peel the transfer tape up, removing the vinyl from its paper backing. Position the transfer tape over your llama where the vinyl design should be laid. Push the transfer tape down onto the llama and run the brayer tool or scraper over the design. Carefully peel up the transfer tape, leaving your design on the llama. Repeat with each piece of the design.

Step 6.

Step 7: Add any extra embellishments to your llama that you would like, then glue your llama to the mason jar using your hot glue gun.

Step 7.

Fill your llama with your favorite craft supplies and tools. It makes the cutest little desktop organizer!

"Wish Upon a Star" Basswood Wall Decor

Cricut Maker Project

Do you still believe in the magic of wishing upon stars? You will after you create this beautiful piece of wall decor! In our last project, you learned how to add color to basswood or chipboard using paint; in this project. I'm showing you how to add color using iron-on or vinyl! Iron-on isn't just for clothing (as you learned in our iron-on section). I love using it for other things, and applying it to wood or chipboard is such a fun application! I wanted to give this project a lot of depth, so I'm having you cut out the word *wish* twice and layer them together using glue so that the word sticks out quite a bit from the star background. This project would look adorable on a nursery wall or used to decorate the room of anyone who needs a reminder of the magic that comes from wishing upon stars!

Materials:

- "Wish Upon A Star" cut file
- 2 pieces Cricut basswood, 11 x 11 inches
- StrongGrip cutting mat
- Masking or painter's tape
- Cricut knife blade
- Vinyl or iron-on in the color you would like the star and the word *wish*
- Regular grip cutting mat
- Fine-tip cutting blade
- Glue
- Weeding tools
- Transfer tape (if using vinyl)
- Brayer or scraper
- Heavy book
- Cricut EasyPress or iron (if using iron-on)

Directions:

Note: Make sure to read Cricut Maker Knife Blade Success Tips on page 157 of this book for best cutting results.

Step 1: Log into Cricut Design Space and upload the "Wish Upon A Star" cut file following the Cut File Upload instructions on page 28 of this book.

Step 2: Size your design so that your star is 10 inches wide by clicking on it and using either the arrow that appears in the bottom right-hand corner of the design or the Size tool in the top toolbar. Duplicate the star so you have two of them (one cut out of basswood and one cut out of iron-on or vinyl). Change the color of your second star to help you remember to cut it from iron-on or vinyl. Duplicate *wish* so that you have three of them by clicking on it and then pressing the Duplicate button (we're going to layer our basswood so it's two layers thick and then one layer of iron-on or vinyl). Change the color of one *wish* to help you remember to cut it from iron-on or vinyl.

Step 2.

Step 3: Click Make It. Cut one of the stars and two *wish* from basswood using the knife blade. Tape the basswood to the StrongGrip mat using painter's tape or masking tape.

Cut one star and one *wish* out of iron-on or vinyl. Use a regular grip mat and a fine-point blade. If you're using iron-on for any of the pieces, make sure you mirror them using the mirror slider under each mat on the left-hand side of the screen. Remember that iron-on goes color/shiny side down on the cutting mat.

Following the prompts on the screen, load your cutting mat into the machine using the arrow on the right-hand side of your Cricut. Once your mat is loaded, look for the Cricut C to start flashing, press the button, and your machine will start cutting. When your machine finishes cutting, press the arrow again and your mat will unload.

Make sure to follow the "best practices guide" for cutting basswood or chipboard at the beginning of this chapter.

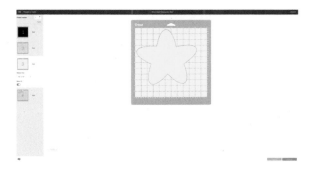

Step 3.

Step 3.

Step 4: Glue your two sets of the word *wish* to each other so it's two layers thick. Put a heavy book on top to press together and dry.

Step 4.

Step 5: Weed your vinyl or iron-on, removing the area around each design, leaving just the design on the paper backing.

Step 5.

Step 6: Once the glue has dried, apply your iron-on or vinyl to your star and *wish* word. If using iron-on, follow the heat temperature suggestions for attaching the type of iron-on you're using to wood. If using vinyl, use transfer tape to transfer your vinyl to each basswood shape.

Step 6.

Step 7: Glue *wish* to the front of your star. Put a heavy book on top and allow the glue to dry.

Step 7.

Attach a Command Strip or other hanger to the back of your star and hang on the wall! Remember the magic of making wishes on stars whenever you see it!

HOME STATE SIGN

I love the look of scroll saw work! There are a ton of artists out there who create amazing home decor pieces with their scroll saws that leave me in awe. I'm a Pacific Northwest girl at heart who grew up in Washington State and now lives in British Columbia. I love the look of scroll-sawed state signs, but I'm also a big fan of using what you have. I decided that before I invested the time and money into a new hobby I would see if I could replicate the look using my Cricut Maker and knife blade. I love how this piece turned out. This project definitely takes a bit of time for your Cricut to cut out, but the finished result is well worth the wait! This home state sign is perfect for using in a family gallery wall and reminding you of all the pride you have for the place where you grew up! Find the cut file for your own home state or province, place a heart in the city where you grew up, and get your Cricut Maker cutting!

Materials:

- Home cut file
- Cut file for your home state or province*
- 2 pieces Cricut basswood, 11 x 11 inches
- 2 pieces Cricut basswood, 6 x 12 inches
- StrongGrip cutting mat
- Masking or painter's tape
- Cricut knife blade
- Paint brushes
- Paint in your favorite colors
- Glue
- Heavy books or clamps

*Cricut has images available for purchase of US states and Canadian provinces. You can also upload your own image to Design Space to cut out.

Directions:

Note: *Make sure to read Cricut Maker Knife Blade Success Tips on page 157 of this book for best cutting results.*

Step 1: Log into Cricut Design Space and upload the "home" cut file following the Cut File Upload instructions on page 28 of this book. Under Images, search for an image of your home state or find your own image of your home state and upload it to Design Space.

Step 2: Press the Shape button in the left-hand toolbar, and select a heart and a square. Size the square so it is 11 inches by 11 inches. Do this by clicking on the square and using either the arrow that appears in the bottom right-hand corner of the design or the Size tool in the top toolbar.

Press the Shape button and select a square. Unlock the size constriction box and create 4 rectangles that are 11 inches by ½ inch and 4 rectangles that are 10 inches by ½ inch. These pieces will be the frame for around your image.

Lay the rectangles that will be your frame over your 11 x 11-inch square. Next, lay your home state over the top of the square along with the word *home* to determine what size you want each piece to be. Play with the sizing until you get a layout that works for you.

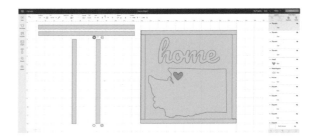

Step 2.

Step 3: Position the heart on your home state so it's over the city you are from. With both the heart and state selected, click Attach. This will make your heart cut where it is laid on the map.

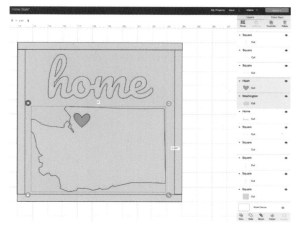

Step 3.

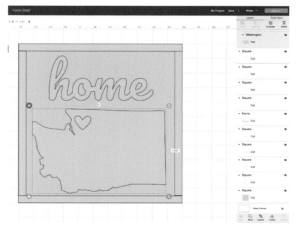

Step 3.

Step 4: Make note of where your home state is positioned on the square, because this is where you'll want the state cut on your piece of basswood or chipboard. Delete the 11 x 11-inch square and then click Make It.

Your home state and the heart will cut from 1 piece of 11 x 11-inch basswood. The second piece of basswood will be used as a backing for your picture frame and won't be cut.

The *home* and 8 pieces of picture frame will be cut from two pieces of 6 x 12-inch basswood.

Use the edit function under the cutting mat where your state is to position your home state on the cutting mat on your screen so it's positioned where you want it to cut from. After your design is cut and painted, you will be fitting the pieces back together like a puzzle, so where your home state cuts from is important. Tape your basswood or chipboard to a StrongGrip mat using painter's tape or masking tape.

Step 4 continued on next page.

Cut your state, the word *home*, and the pieces of frame, making sure to follow the *Cricut Maker Knife Blade Success Tips* for cutting basswood or chipboard at the beginning of this chapter (page 157). Check to make sure that your design has cut all the way through before unloading your mat from your Cricut Maker. If it hasn't cut all the way through, press the Cricut C to have your machine make another pass at the cut. Make sure you do this before you unload the mat from your cutting machine.

Step 4.

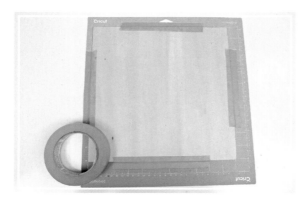

Step 4.

Step 4.

Step 5: Once all the pieces are done cutting, it's time to start painting! Choose a color for each piece and paint them, giving them plenty of time to dry.

Step 6: Once everything is dried, it's time to assemble. Pop the state and the heart into their holes. Next, glue the front piece with your state to the back piece of basswood that you didn't cut. Then assemble your frame. We've cut two pieces of frame for each side of the square to give it a bit of extra depth. Glue the two pieces for each side, stacked one on top of each other, then glue them on top of the square that your state is cut from, creating a frame around the edge of the square. Finally, glue the word *home* to the front of your basswood. Set a heavy book on top of the entire thing to press the glue down while it dries.

Step 5.

Step 6.

Attach a Command Strip or other hanger to the back of your home state decor and hang on the wall! Remember, there's no place like home!

An Introduction to Leather and Faux Leather

Let's Talk Leather!

Leather is one of those unexpected materials that people get really excited about cutting with their Cricut. I can't tell you how many times someone has said to me: "I didn't know the Cricut can cut leather!" Not only *can* the Cricut cut leather, but it can also cut faux leather! Cricut produces a wide range of faux leather in different colors and patterns. In this chapter, we'll be using genuine leather as well as faux leather and faux suede. Feel free to swap genuine leather for faux leather, or faux leather for genuine leather, in any of these projects!

What can you make with leather and faux leather:

- Bracelets
- Earrings
- Bookmarks
- Wallets
- Journal covers
- Tassels
- Scrapbook embellishments
- Keychains
- Pen holders
- And much, much more!

Pro-Crafter Leather Tip

Leather and faux leather makes an excellent "blank canvas"! Think of different ways you can embellish your project by adding vinyl, HTV, and foiling to your project. Make sure you take a peek at our Foil Quill Faux Leather Lip Balm Holder on page 275 of this book for instructions on how to foil on faux leather!

Other Useful Tools & Materials for Working with Leather and Faux Leather

- **Deep-point blade:** This is my favorite blade for cutting leather with my Cricut. Bonus: you can use it in both the Cricut Maker and the Cricut Explore!
- **StrongGrip cutting mat:** I can't tell you how frustrating it is to have your leather slip off the mat when it's halfway through cutting. A StrongGrip mat combined with a brayer tool will help make sure your leather stays in place while cutting.
- **Brayer tools:** My brayer tool is something I use way more than I originally expected to. Place your leather onto your StrongGrip cutting mat and then run the brayer over the top to really push all areas of the leather onto the cutting mat to make sure it stays in place.
- **Jewelry tools:** I use my jewelry toolset quite often when working with leather. Having a tool for punching holes in leather along with a set of jewelry pliers will make leather jewelry–making easy!

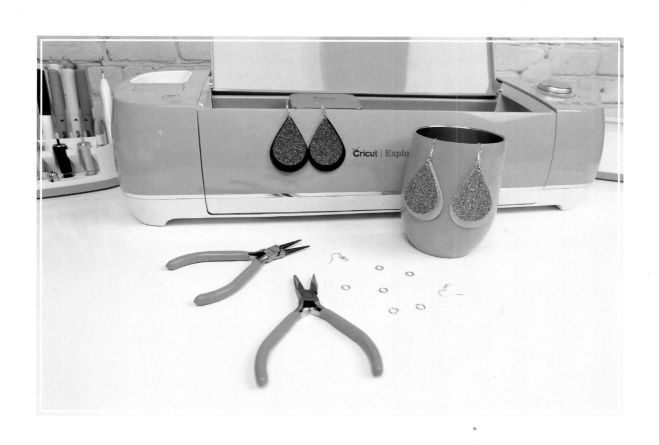

DIY Leather Headphones Keeper

Cricut Explore **or** Cricut Maker Project

I still remember when I found out that I could cut leather with my Cricut; it was like a whole new world had opened up to me! You can make so many fun things with leather (or faux leather)! Bracelets, earrings, keychains, journals, wallets, and more! This project idea came to me out of a need that I kept running into in my life. I love taking headphones with me when I leave the house. I never know when I'll have a few spare minutes to listen to a podcast or watch Netflix when the kids are at their activities, when I've stopped at a café, or when I'm traveling. I usually throw my headphones into my purse, a zippered pouch, or my jacket pocket and I find that every single time I take them back out, they're a tangled mess. These little cord-keepers will keep your headphones knot-free, plus they are super cute, too! Make one for yourself, give them as gifts (they make a great present for a hard-to-buy-for teen), and keep the headache of tangled cords at bay!

Materials:

- Headphones Keeper cut file
- Cricut leather or faux leather in your favorite color
- StrongGrip cutting mat
- Brayer tool
- Deep-point Blade
- Snap hole tool
- Snaps with an extra-long post if using leather, or regular length for using faux leather
- Snap press

Directions:

Step 1: Log into Cricut Design Space and upload the Headphones Keeper cut file following the Cut File Upload instructions on page 28 of this book.

Step 2: Size your design to 6.5 inches wide by clicking on the design and using either the arrow that appears in the bottom right-hand corner of the design or the Size tool in the top toolbar.

Step 2.

Step 3: Click Make It. Set your cutting material to the type of leather you're using. Load your deep-point blade into your Cricut. Lay leather shiny side down on your cutting mat. Use your brayer tool to push the leather down onto the mat. Load your cutting mat into your Cricut using the arrow on the right-hand side of your Cricut. Once your mat is loaded, look for the Cricut C to start flashing, press the button, and your machine will start cutting.

When your machine has finished cutting, before using the arrow to unload the mat, make sure that your design has cut all the way through. If it hasn't, then press the Cricut C to have your Cricut repeat the cut. When your machine finishes cutting, and you're satisfied that your design is cut all the way through, press the arrow again and your mat will unload.

Step 3.

Step 4: Peel your leather design off the cutting mat. Fold in the three corners of your triangle. Use your snap hole tool to punch a hole where your snap goes and then add snaps to your headphone keeper using your snap press.

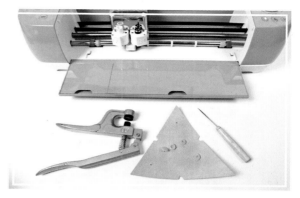

Step 4.

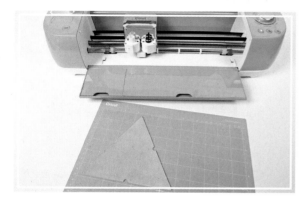

Step 4.

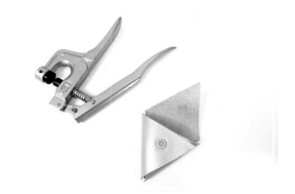

Stick your headphones inside the headphone keeper and enjoy tangle-free headphones!

10-Minute Leather Heart "Mom" Keychain

Cricut Explore **or** Cricut Maker Project

Being a mom is the best—and the hardest—job in the entire world. If you're a mom, you're well aware of that fact. This mama doesn't have time to mess around! I love creating beautiful things in as little time as possible, and if you're like me, then this project won't disappoint! We're making a DIY Leather Heart *Mom* Keychain! This project is so quick and easy, it could probably be done in five minutes . . . but I'm going to say ten just to be on the safe side! Pop your deep-point blade into your Cricut Maker or Cricut Explore and let's get crafting!

Materials:

- Mom Keychain cut file
- Cricut leather in your 2 favorite colors
- StrongGrip cutting mat
- Brayer tool
- Deep-point blade
- Black iron-on
- Regular grip cutting mat
- Fine-tip blade
- Weeding tools
- Iron-on protective sheet
- EasyPress or iron
- E6000 glue
- Key ring
- Something heavy like a stack of books

Directions:

Step 1: Log into Cricut Design Space and upload the Mom Keychain cut file following the Cut File Upload instructions on page 28 of this book.

Step 2: Size your design to 5 inches wide by clicking on the design and using either the arrow that appears in the bottom right-hand corner of the design or the Size tool in the top toolbar.

Note: I like making two of these keychains at one time with two different colors of leather. When I cut two at once, I delete the small heart, because I use the small heart that's cut from the center of the big heart on the opposite color of leather keychain.

Step 2.

Step 3: Click Make It. The heart pieces get cut out of leather. Set your cutting material to the type of leather you're using. Load your deep-point blade into your Cricut. Lay the leather shiny side down on your StrongGrip cutting mat. Use your brayer tool to push the leather down onto the mat. Load your cutting mat into your Cricut using the arrow on the right-hand side of your Cricut. Once your mat is loaded,

look for the Cricut C to start flashing, press the button, and your machine will start cutting.

When your machine has finished cutting, before using the arrow to unload the mat, make sure your design has cut all the way through. If it hasn't, then press the Cricut C to have your Cricut repeat the cut. When your machine finishes cutting, and you're satisfied that your design is cut all the way through, press the arrow again and your mat will unload.

The "M M" piece gets cut from black iron-on with the shiny black side down on a regular grip cutting mat. Don't forget to mirror your image using the mirror slider under the mat on the left-hand side. Make sure you set your cut setting to the type of iron-on you're using.

Step 3.

Step 3.

Step 4: Weed your iron-on, leaving just the "M M" on the clear plastic backing.

Step 4.

Step 5: Pop the small leather heart inside of the big leather heart. Lay your iron-on on top of the main piece of your keychain. The small leather heart should be centered between the two Ms. Lay the Cricut Protective Iron-On Sheet over your leather and iron-on, and press using your iron or your Cricut EasyPress set at 280°F for 30 seconds. Check to make sure that your iron-on is adhered to the leather and then slowly peel away the clear plastic cover.

Step 5.

Step 6: Fold your heart in half and slide the key ring over it, positioning the ring on the rectangular area that connects the two hearts. Lay the leather with the side with "mom" on it facing down. Use your E6000 glue to glue the two sides of the keychain together. Pinch shut and wipe away any glue that might spill out the edges. Put the keychain under a stack of heavy books for twenty-four hours so the glue has time to cure.

Step 6.

Give your mom this keychain to let her know that she's always in your heart.

DIY Leather Teardrop Earrings

Cricut Explore or Cricut Maker Project

If you love making handmade gifts for your friends, you're going to love this project! Not only are they sparkly and fun, but they're also inexpensive to make! You can easily make eleven pairs of earrings out of one sheet of leather and one roll of HTV! These pretty earrings would be perfect for party favors, teacher gifts, bridesmaid gifts, and "just because" presents for friends! Play around with making the earrings in different sizes, in different colors of leather, and with different finishes of HTV. You can also make these earrings with faux leather to make those crafting dollars go even farther!

Materials:

- Teardrop Earring cut file
- Cricut leather in your favorite color
- Deep-point blade
- StrongGrip cutting mat
- Brayer tool
- HTV in your favorite color/finish (we used glitter iron-on)
- Regular grip cutting mat
- Fine-point blade
- Leather tool, needle, or safety pin
- Jewelry pliers
- Jump rings (2 rings for each pair of earrings)
- Earring hooks

Directions:

Step 1: Log into Cricut Design Space and upload the Teardrop Earrings cut file following the Cut File Upload instructions on page 28 of this book.

Step 2: Size your earrings to the size that you would like them to cut at. To do this, click on the design and use the arrow that appears in the bottom right-hand corner to size your earrings. Four of the teardrops will be cut out of leather. Cut two of the smaller teardrops out of iron-on.

Step 2.

Step 3: Click Make It. Set your cutting material to the type of leather you're using. Load your deep-point blade into your Cricut. Lay leather shiny side down on your StrongGrip cutting mat. Use your brayer tool to push the leather down onto the mat. Load your cutting mat into your Cricut using the arrow on the right-hand side of your Cricut. Once your mat is loaded, look for the Cricut C to start flashing, press the button, and your machine will start cutting. Unload your leather mat from your Cricut. Cut HTV using a fine-tip blade. Lay the HTV with the shiny colored side facing down on a regular grip cutting mat. Set your Cricut to the

type of iron-on you're using. Mirror your design using the mirror slider on the cutting mat on the left-hand side of the screen.

When your machine has finished cutting, before using the arrow to unload the mat, make sure your design has cut all the way through. If it hasn't, then press the Cricut C to have your Cricut repeat the cut. When your machine finishes cutting, and you're satisfied that your design is cut all the way through, press the arrow again and your mat will unload.

Step 3.

Step 4: Weed your iron-on, removing the area surrounding the earring design, leaving just the teardrops on the plastic backing.

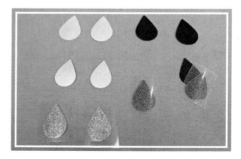

Step 4.

Step 5: Heat your EasyPress or iron. Lay your glitter iron-on on top of the leather piece that is the same size. Press using the instructions for the type of iron-on you're using. I pressed at 270°F for 20 seconds.

Step 6.

Step 5.

Step 6: Use a leather tool, needle, or safety pin to punch a hole near the top of each teardrop. Use jewelry pliers to loop a jump ring through the hole you've punched in the leather and then attach the jump ring to your earring hook.

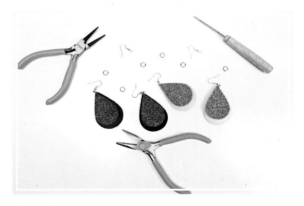

Step 6.

You've created a beautiful pair of leather earrings! What kind of earrings can you make next? Think about the different shapes you could make out of the leather and how you could decorate them. How would patterned iron-on look? You could also "draw" on your leather with your Cricut Maker and a debossing tip.

DIY "Create A Beautiful Life" Journal Cover

Cricut Explore **or** Cricut Maker Project

I love taking something simple and inexpensive that I find at the dollar store and turning it into something amazing! In this project, I'm teaching you how to turn a simple dollar-store notebook into a beautiful leather journal perfect for using as a travel journal, to keep track of goals, or as an everyday diary. We're using a wood grain faux leather in this project, but you could also use regular leather. To give this leather a beautiful, one-of-a-kind look, we're going to add an HTV decal to the front that says "Create A Beautiful Life." You could also leave the front of the cover plain, use a quote of your own, or even add a monogram! Play around with different colors and finishes of faux leather or leather to give this journal a look and feel that's as 100 percent as unique as you are!

Materials:

- Journal Cover and Create a Beautiful Life cut files
- 2 pieces Cricut faux leather in your favorite color and finish (we used a wood grain faux leather)*
- Regular grip cutting mat
- Fine-point blade
- HTV in your favorite color
- Weeding tools
- Wonder clips or bulldog clips
- Sewing machine
- Coordinating thread
- EasyPress or iron
- EasyPress Mat or a towel to protect your work surface

*One piece will be used for the outside cover and the other piece for the inside flaps.

Directions:

Step 1: Log into Cricut Design Space and upload the Journal Cover and Create a Beautiful Life cut files, following the Cut File Upload instructions on page 28 of this book.

Step 2: Measure your journal. Click on each journal piece and size it. For the big piece, you'll want to measure the width of your journal, double it, and add 1 inch. For the height, you'll want to measure the height of your journal and add 1 inch. For the two small pieces, change the height so they're the same height as the big journal cover piece. For my project, I opted to have the outside of my journal one color and the inside flaps a second color.

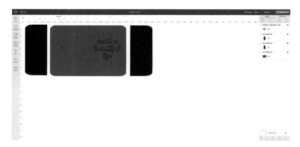

Step 2.

Step 3: Click Make It. Set your cutting material to the type of faux leather you're using. Lay your faux leather on your cutting mat. Load your cutting mat into your Cricut using the arrow on the right-hand side of your Cricut. Once your mat is loaded, look for the Cricut C to start flashing, press the button, and your machine will start cutting. Press the arrow button again once your Cricut has finished cutting to unload the mat.

Cut iron-on with color side facing down on the mat. Set your Cricut to iron-on when cutting and mirror your design using the mirror slider on the cutting mat on the left-hand side of the screen.

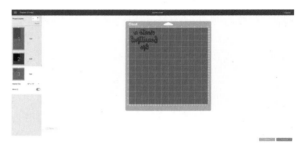

Step 3.

Step 3.

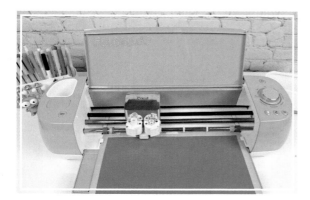

Step 3.

Step 4: Lay your large piece of faux leather on your work surface with the finished side facing down. Lay your two smaller pieces of faux leather on top of the large piece with the finished side facing up. Line up one piece on the right and the other piece on the left. Clip into place.

Step 4.

Step 5: Use your sewing machine to sew all the way around your journal cover using a ⅛-inch seam allowance. Make sure to backstitch when you start sewing and again at the end.

Step 5.

Step 6: Weed your iron-on, removing the area surrounding the words, leaving just the design on the plastic backing. Don't forget to weed the inside of the letters, as well (for example, inside the e, a, f, etc.).

Step 6.

Step 7: Heat your EasyPress or iron to the temperature recommended for the iron-on you're using. Lay your iron-on where you would like it placed on your journal cover. Press using the instructions for the type of iron-on you are using.

Step 7.

Step 8: Slip the front and back covers of your journal inside the flaps of your journal cover.

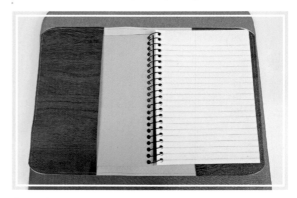

Step 8.

You've turned an inexpensive journal into a thing of beauty. Feel inspired each time you write in it! I'd love to see your journal covers! Share them with me on Instagram and make sure to use the hashtag #hcfcricutcrafts and tag @hellocreativefamily!

"I Like Big Books and I Cannot Lie" Tasseled Faux Suede Bookmark

Cricut Explore **or** Cricut Maker Project

One of the reasons why becoming a published author has been so exciting for me is that books have always been a big part of my life. As a child, I was a *huge* bookworm. When I was a teenager, my dad told me that I should be an author when I grew up. In my early twenties, I worked at a bookstore (and that's where I met my husband!). In my late twenties and thirties, I worked as a children's book publicist. And finally, in my late thirties, I became an author! My two children are big book lovers, too. They constantly have their noses buried in books and, much to my chagrin, they're constantly leaving books lying around the house on the couch, side tables, beds, and counters. Bookmarks are a hot commodity in my house, so I decided to create this beautiful faux suede tasseled bookmark. It has a fun little quote on it, because even the most sophisticated bookmark needs to let its hair down every once in a while and have some fun.

Materials:

- I Like Big Books and I Cannot Lie Tasseled Bookmark cut file
- Black iron-on
- Regular grip cutting mat
- Fine-point blade
- Cricut Faux Suede (or your favorite faux leather or genuine leather)
- Brayer
- Deep-point blade*
- Weeding tools
- EasyPress or iron
- EasyPress Mat or a towel to protect your work surface
- Glue gun

*You can also use a regular tip blade, but I find that the deep-point blade does a better job with the faux suede.

Directions:

Step 1: Log into Cricut Design Space and upload the I Like Big Books and I Cannot Lie Tasseled Bookmark cut file following the Cut File Upload instructions on page 28 of this book.

Step 2: Size your bookmark by clicking on the design and using the arrow button in the bottom right-hand corner. You can also play with the tassel size and the size of the leather strip that attaches the tassel to the bookmark.

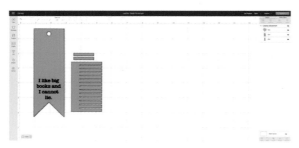

Step 2.

Step 3: Click Make It. Mirror the cutting mat with the words by using the mirror slider on the cutting mat on the left-hand side of the screen. Set your cutting material to the type of iron-on you're using. Lay your iron-on on your cutting mat with the color shiny side facing down. Load your cutting mat into your Cricut using the arrow on the right-hand side of your Cricut. Once your mat is loaded, look for the Cricut C to start flashing, press the button, and your machine will start cutting. Press the arrow button again once your Cricut has finished cutting to unload the mat.

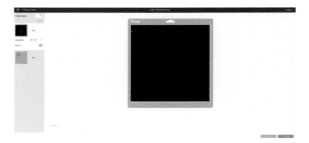

Step 3.

Lay your faux leather on your cutting mat. Use your brayer to make sure the faux leather is pushed firmly down onto the cutting mat. Set your material type to the type of faux leather you're using. Switch the blade in your machine to the deep-point blade and switch the blade type on your screen to match. Load your cutting mat into your Cricut using the arrow on the right-hand side of your Cricut. Once your mat is loaded, look for the Cricut C to start flashing, press the button, and your machine will start cutting. Before ejecting your mat, make sure your faux leather is cut all the way through. If it is, press the arrow button to unload your mat. If it's not cut all the way through, press the flashing Cricut C to get your machine to make another pass with the blade.

Step 4: Weed your iron-on, removing the area surrounding the words, leaving just the design on the plastic backing. Don't forget to weed the inside of the letters, as well (for example, inside the b, g, o, etc).

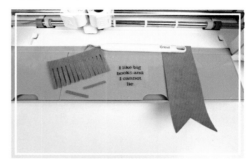

Step 4.

Step 5: Heat your EasyPress or iron to the temperature recommended for the iron-on you're using. Lay your iron-on where you would like it placed on your bookmark. Press using the instructions for the type of iron-on you're using.

Step 3.

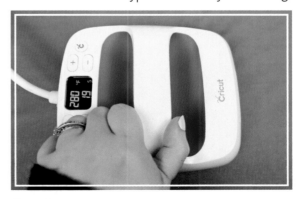

Step 5.

Step 6: Heat your glue gun. Loop one of the long, thin strips of faux leather through the hole of your bookmark. Attach the two ends of the strip to each other by lining up the two ends, with the right side of the faux leather facing out, and securing in place with a drop of hot glue. You've just created the strap that will connect to the inside of your tassel.

Lay your tassel piece on your work surface, with the fringe of your tassel toward the right and the solid strip toward the left. Place a drop of hot glue at the end of your strap that you just made and lay it in the bottom corner of the solid strip of tassel. Add another drop of glue to the top of the strap and then roll up your tassel, wrapping the solid strip around the strap. When you get to the end, put a drop of hot glue to attach it.

Take your final strip of faux leather and wrap it around the top of the tassel and hot glue it in place.

And there you have it! A beautiful faux suede bookmark! This project is so fun, and the cut file can be used in a ton of different ways! Make the bookmark out of real leather, felt, or even paper! Create your own DIY tassels out of different materials like yarn and ribbon. Create tassels in different sizes to hang from purses, keychains, and as zipper pulls! What other quotes can you think of to put on your bookmark? Feeling inspired by this project? Make sure to share your bookmark projects with me on Instagram by tagging #HCFCricutCrafts and @hellocreativefamily!

Step 6.

Step 6.

An Introduction to Infusible Ink

Infusible Ink is Cricut's version of sublimation—and it is AMAZING! At the time this book is being written, there are two ways to use Infusible Ink.

- **Infusible Ink Pens:** Use these pens to draw on laser copy paper either by hand or by using the pen attachment on your Cricut. Next, use heat to infuse the design into one of Cricut's Infusible Ink blanks.
- **Infusible Ink Transfer Sheets:** Think of Infusible Ink Transfer Sheets like you would iron-on. Use your Cricut to cut a design on the Infusible Ink Transfer Sheet, weed your project, and then use heat to infuse the design directly into one of Cricut's Infusible Ink Blanks.

Cricut Infusible Ink Blanks Available:

- Shirts
- Onesies
- Tote bags
- Coasters

Can I use Infusible Ink on my own blanks?

This is one of the most common questions I get asked about Infusible Ink. Can you? Sure! Should you? That's a different question. Cricut put a lot of time and science into developing Infusible Ink. The shirts, onesies, coasters, and totes are all made of materials that have been specifically created to give you the best, longest lasting results every single time you use them. Infusible Ink will not absorb into regular blank tiles. You may be able to get Infusible Ink to infuse into other fabric blanks; however, most people have reported that the color isn't as vibrant and the longevity of the design isn't very good.

How is Infusible Ink different from iron-on?

Infusible Ink Transfer Sheets and iron-on are very similar in many ways. With both, you select a design, mirror the design, lay your sheet color-side down on the cutting mat, cut, weed, and use heat to transfer. The biggest difference is your finished result. Infusible Ink is permanently infused into your blank. It becomes one with your material! Because it's infused into the blank, that means that it's seamless! When you run your hand over your blank, it will feel flat. There's no difference by touch from where the ink is infused and where it isn't. Since the Infusible Ink becomes one with the blank there's no flaking, no peeling, no cracking, and no wrinkling—ever! It really is like magic.

> **Pro-Crafter Tip**
> Infusible Ink needs a high, consistent, even dry heat to infuse. The coasters, for example, need an even heat of 400°F for 240 seconds. Because of this, a Cricut EasyPress really is necessary to achieve your desired results.

Infusible Ink Lingo

Curious about the different terms people are throwing around when talking about Cricut Crafts? We've got you covered!

Sublimation Printing: This is a term you may hear often when talking to others about Infusible Ink. *Sublimation* is a chemical process where a solid turns into a gas without going through a liquid stage. *Sublimation printing* is a method of transferring images onto different materials like T-shirts and bags. Sublimation printing involves a chemical reaction and fancy equipment. Infusible Ink is Cricut's version of sublimation printing, created to make the process easy for your average crafter.

Weeding: The process of removing the negative space around your design. So, for example, if you have your Cricut cut an "O," you would need to remove the excess HTV from around the outside of your O and the inside of your O, leaving just the letter itself on the plastic backing.

Mirror: To flip or reverse an image. You do this when using Infusible Ink because you apply the ink to the shirt with the color side facing down onto your blank.

Kiss cut: To cut through just the first layer of a material, not all the way through. A kiss cut is used with Infusible Ink Transfer Sheets. It means that your machine will just cut the transfer sheet and not the plastic backing. This is something that your Cricut will do automatically for you when set to the correct material setting.

Heat Press: A machine used to heat your Infusible Ink and make it infuse into the material you're adding your design to.

Other Useful Tools & Materials for Working with Infusible Ink

- **Cardstock:** Infusible Ink projects that involve fabric (shirts, onesies, and tote bags) will have you put a piece of cardstock inside of the blank so that the Infusible Ink doesn't sink through to the back of your project.
- **Butcher paper:** Cricut recommends putting a protective layer of butcher paper between your EasyPress and your design to help prevent ink from staining your heat press and to provide an extra protective layer.
- **Laser Copy Paper:** Draw designs on laser copy paper by hand, or by using your Cricut's draw function, and then transfer them to an Infusible Ink blank using high temperature heat. This only works with laser copy paper because it holds up to the high temperature.
- **Lint roller:** Lint, dust, and hair are an Infusible Ink project's worst enemy. A lint roller comes in handy to make sure any little bits and pieces have been removed from your blank so you get the best Infusible Ink results.
- **Fine-tip cutting blade:** This is your go-to blade for cutting Infusible Ink Transfer Sheets and most regular materials like vinyl, cardstock, scrapbook paper, and more. (See the materials list at the beginning of the book for which blades you will need for different types of materials, page 7.)
- **Regular grip cutting mat:** A regular grip cutting mat has the perfect grip for keeping your Infusible Ink designs secure while cutting.
- **Weeding tools:** Weeding tools help you remove the "negative space" from in and around your design. It's especially helpful when weeding small letters and intricate designs. You also use weeding tools with vinyl, HTV, and paper.
- **Cricut EasyPress or Heat Press:** The Cricut EasyPress is available in four sizes all the way from an itty bitty EasyPress Mini to a 12 x 10-inch press that's perfect for larger designs. Heat presses and EasyPresses have even heat signatures, precise temperature control, and an even pressure that helps you get flawless results.
- **EasyPress Mat:** This handy little mat isn't just for protecting your work surface from heat (though it does that too!). It has a special inner liner that wicks moisture to deliver clean, dry heat, and a foil membrane that reflects heat to your project.

INFUSIBLE INK SUCCULENT COASTERS

Cricut Explore **or** Cricut Maker Project (Cricut Joy Compatible)

One of my very favorite things to watch my Cricut do is draw. I love putting a pen in the pen holder and watching the Cricut sketch out a design. When Cricut came out with their Infusible Ink coaster blanks, I knew I wanted my kids make their own coasters. I had my Cricut draw out some "coloring pages" and had my kids color them in using Infusible Ink pens. Then I let them pick their favorites to put onto coasters. My daughter made a succulent coaster for her first coaster that I absolutely love, so I decided for this project to draw a collection of succulents for you that you can turn into coasters of your own. I drew three succulents and gave you a fourth "succulent pot" that's empty inside so you can draw in your very own succulent!

Materials:

- Succulent drawing files
- Infusible Ink pens
- Laser copy paper
- LightGrip cutting mat
- Fine-tip blade
- Cricut EasyPress 2
- Cricut EasyPress Mat
- Cardstock
- Infusible Ink blank coasters
- Lint roller
- Cricut Heat Resistant Tape
- Butcher paper

Directions:

Step 1: Log into Cricut Design Space and use the **Shape** tool to create 4 circles that are each 3.5 inches wide. Upload the succulents drawing files using the instructions on page 28 of this book.

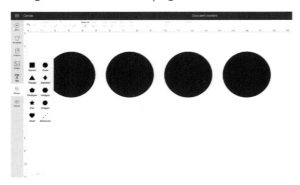

Step 1.

Step 2: Size the succulents to 3.25 x 3.25 inches and change the line type to **Draw**.

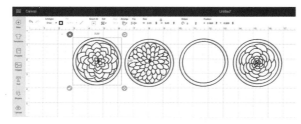

Step 2.

Step 3: Center one succulent drawing on the top of each of the circles. Making sure that both the succulent and circle are selected, hit **Attach**. Do this for all four succulents.

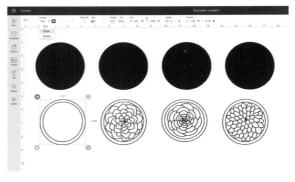

Step 3.

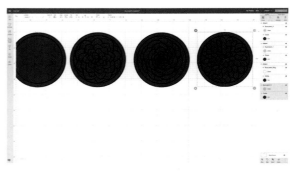

Step 3.

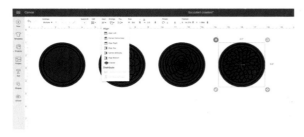

Step 3.

Step 4: Click Make It. Change your material size to 8.5 x 11 inches. Slide the mirror slider to mirror your image.

> ### Pro-Crafter Tip
> Mirroring your project won't do much for this project since it doesn't matter what direction the design is in, but it's a good habit to get into for when you're working with designs where direction matters, like with writing.

Step 5: Select Laser Copy Paper as your cutting material. Load your Infusible Ink Pen into your machine, lay a piece of laser copy paper on your cutting mat and load it into your machine, Click the cute little Cricut C on your machine to start cutting! Sit back and watch your Cricut draw.

Step 6: Gently remove your succulent circles from the cutting mat. Use your Infusible Ink Pens to color them in.

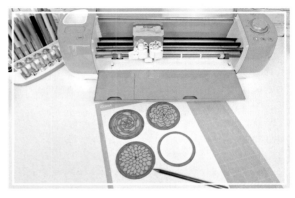

Step 6.

> ### Pro-Crafter Tip
> Don't be fooled if the color on the paper appears darker than you expect, especially when wet. The color of the plastic marker itself is the color your infused ink will be!

Step 7: Set the temperature of your Cricut EasyPress 2 to 400°F and the timer to 240 seconds. Lay out your EasyPress Mat and cover it with a piece of cardstock.

Set your coaster on your EasyPress Mat with the shiny side facing up. Use a lint roller or a lint-free cloth to wipe any dust or lint from your coaster. Don't skip this step—it's an important one to make sure your design infuses into the coaster properly.

Lay your design onto your coaster with the colored side facing down. Use your Cricut Heat Resistant Tape to tape the design into place.

Flip your coaster so the design is facing down, cover your coaster with butcher paper, and press using your Cricut EasyPress 2. Do not move the EasyPress around. Keep it as still as possible with firm, steady pressure.

When your EasyPress beeps that the timer is done, slowly lift your EasyPress, being careful not to disrupt the coaster. Your coaster is going to be VERY HOT, so don't touch it. Leave it alone until your coaster is cool to the touch.

Remove the tape and paper and reveal your design!

Step 7.

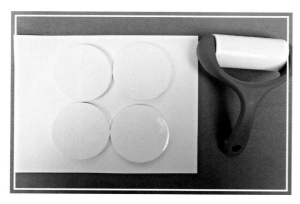

Step 7.

Step 7.

The possibilities really are endless with these coasters. As long as you have Infusible Ink Pens and laser copy paper, you can draw anything you want to transfer onto the coasters. You can also cut designs out of Cricut Infusible Ink Transfer Sheets to be put onto coasters. Make sure you check out our Food & Drink Coasters on page 241 of this book to learn how to use Infusible Ink Transfer Sheets on coasters!

"Homegrown" Infusible Ink Onesie

Cricut Explore **or** Cricut Maker Project (Cricut Joy Compatible)

Let's be honest . . . kids' clothes get put through the wringer! From spit up, baby food, and blowouts on onesies to PB&J smears, grass stains, and mud pie splatters on toddler clothes. You don't truly get to know just how much of a time suck laundry can be until you become a parent. HTV can eventually peel after a lot of washes, and that's one of the reasons I love Infusible Ink for kids' clothing! Since Infusible Ink infuses right into the clothing, there's no risk of the design peeling after a million and one washes. For this "Homegrown" Infusible Ink onesie, we're using a simple design and letting the Infusible Ink Transfer Sheet really shine! I loved being pregnant with my kids and thought there was something so magical about the fact that I was growing a little human inside of me. I also love to garden, so I thought that creating a onesie that said "homegrown" in a beautiful floral design was perfect. Cricut makes a ton of incredible designs of Infusible Ink Transfer

Sheets so make sure to check them all out and see where your creative imagination takes you! Also, don't forget that you can use the Infusible Ink pens to make shirts like the Monster Family Portrait project on page 229 of this book!

Materials:

- Homegrown cut file
- Infusible Ink baby onesie
- Measuring tape
- Regular grip cutting mat
- Fine-tip blade
- Cricut floral Infusible Ink transfer sheet from Shaylee collection
- Weeding tools
- Cricut EasyPress Mat
- Cardstock
- Lint roller
- Butcher paper
- Cricut EasyPress 2
- Optional: Brayer tool and heat-safe tape

Directions:

Step 1: Log into Cricut Design Space and upload the Homegrown cut file using the Cut File Upload instructions on page 28 of this book.

Step 2: Measure your onesie to determine how big you want your design to be. Size your design accordingly by clicking on the design and using either the arrow sizer in the corner, or the **Size** tool in the upper toolbar.

Step 2.

Step 3: Click **Make It**. Slide the mirror slider on the cutting mat. Lay your Infusible Ink Transfer Sheet on your cutting mat with the color facing up and liner facing down. I like rolling a brayer over the top of my transfer sheet to make sure it's really pushed down onto the cutting mat and won't shift while cutting. Choose your cutting material, load your cutting mat into your machine using the arrow button, and then click the cute little Cricut C on your machine to start cutting! When your machine is done cutting, press the arrow again to unload the mat.

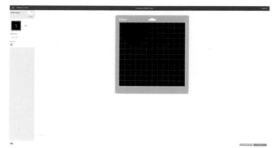

Step 3.

Step 3.

Step 4: Weed the design, removing the excess transfer sheet from around your design, leaving just your design on the clear plastic backing. You will want to remove the area around the heart and then each of the letters, leaving the letter centers in place.

Note that the transfer sheet material is lighter than it will appear once pressed.

Step 4.

Step 5: Heat your Cricut EasyPress to 385°F. Place your onesie on top of your Cricut EasyPress Mat and then put a piece of cardstock inside of your onesie to prevent the Infusible Ink from bleeding through to the back.

Use your lint roller to remove any lint, hair, or dust particles from your onesie.

Lay a piece of butcher paper on top of your onesie and heat for 15 seconds. Do not skip this step. Heating the onesie removes any moisture from the material and allows the Infusible Ink to properly infuse into the fabric and works like magic!

Remove the butcher paper and lay your design where you would like it on your onesie. Lay your butcher paper back on top of the onesie and then press using your EasyPress for 40 seconds. Use steady pressure and be careful to not slide the EasyPress or move your hands around while it's being pressed. You want your EasyPress to remain still with firm pressure. At the end of the 40 seconds, carefully lift the EasyPress and leave your onesie with the butcher paper on top of the design to cool.

Once your design has cooled, lift the butcher paper and carefully peel up the plastic liner, revealing your design!

Step 5.

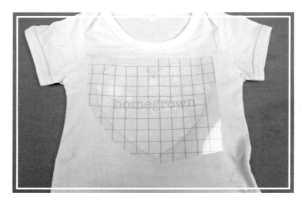

Step 5.

Note: If the transfer sheet doesn't come up with the plastic backer, use a pair of tweezers to carefully lift it up.

Machine wash in cold water inside out with mild detergent. Tumble dry low or line dry. Do not use fabric softener, dryer sheets, or bleach.

Step 5.

This sweet little onesie makes a super cute baby shower gift! Make a whole set of Infusible Ink onesies with different patterns of transfer sheets and designs! Share your creations on Instagram and tag #hcfcricutcrafts and @hellocreativefamily! I'd love to see them.

Monster Family Portrait Infusible Ink "Color Me In" Shirt

Cricut Explore **or** Cricut Maker Project (Cricut Joy Compatible)

We've used Infusible Ink transfer sheets on a onesie, and Infusible Ink pens on a coaster, and now we're going to combine the Infusible Ink pens and transfer sheets into one awesome shirt! I love doodling on my iPad. It makes me so happy to see one of *my* drawings drawn by my Cricut cutting machine! In this project, I'm going to show you how to take a doodle made on a tablet and have your Cricut draw it using a black Infusible Ink pen to turn it into a coloring sheet. It's a super cute monster family portrait that will appeal to kids of all ages. Once it's colored in, we're going to apply it to a shirt (though it would also look super cute on a square coaster or tote bag) and then we're going to add a "frame" made out of an Infusible Ink Transfer Sheet. This project is so fun and is a great way to get your kids involved in crafting!

Materials:

- Monster Family Portrait and Frame cut files
- Infusible Ink shirt
- Measuring tape
- Laser copy paper
- LightGrip cutting mat
- Fine-tip blade
- Cricut Infusible Ink Transfer Sheet for frame
- Regular grip cutting mat
- Weeding tools
- Cricut Infusible Ink pens
- Cricut EasyPress Mat
- Cardstock
- Lint roller
- Butcher paper
- Cricut EasyPress 2
- Optional: Brayer tool and Cricut Heat Resistant Tape

Directions:

Step 1: Log into Cricut Design Space and upload the Monster Family Portrait and Frame cut files using the Cut File Upload instructions on page 28 of this book for uploading PNGs. Change the cut type of the monster family to **Draw** under Linetype in the upper left-hand toolbar.

Step 1.

Step 2: Measure your shirt to determine how big you want your design to be. Select both pieces of the cut file and then use the arrow sizer in the corner to size your design appropriately. Use the **Duplicate** button to copy the picture frame piece. Lay the monster family photo on top of one of the picture frames, sized to the way you would like it. Select both pieces and then click **Slice**. Delete the frame that you just used to slice and the outside edges that have been trimmed off your monster family portrait. You're now ready to draw and cut your monsters and frame.

Step 2.

Step 2.

Step 3: Click **Make It**. Slide the mirror slider on each cutting mat. Load your LightGrip mat with a piece of laser copy paper. Put a black Infusible Ink pen into the pen holder on your machine. Set your cutting material to laser copy paper, load your cutting mat into your machine using the arrow button, and then click the cute little Cricut C on your machine to start cutting! When your machine is done cutting, press the arrow again to unload the mat.

Next, lay your Infusible Ink Transfer Sheet on your regular grip cutting mat with the color facing up and liner facing down. I like rolling a brayer over the top of my transfer sheet to make sure it's really pushed down onto the cutting mat and won't shift while cutting. Change your cutting material in Design Space to Infusible Ink Transfer Sheet. Load your cutting mat into your machine using the arrow button and then click the cute little Cricut C on your machine to start cutting! When your machine is done cutting, press the arrow again to unload the mat.

Step 3.

Step 4: Weed your Infusible Ink Transfer Sheet, removing the excess transfer sheet around the outside and inside of your frame. Note that the transfer sheet material is lighter than it will appear once pressed.

Step 5: Color in your monster family portrait coloring sheet using Infusible Ink pens.

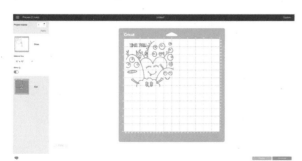

Step 3.

Step 5.

Step 6: Heat your Cricut EasyPress to 385°F. Place your Infusible Ink T-shirt on top of your Cricut EasyPress Mat and then put a piece of cardstock inside the shirt to prevent the Infusible Ink from bleeding through to the back.

Use your lint roller to remove any lint, hair, or dust particles from your T-shirt.

Lay a piece of butcher paper on top of your T-shirt and heat for 15 seconds. Do not skip this step. Heating the shirt removes any moisture from the fabric and allows the Infusible Ink to properly infuse and work its magic!

Remove the butcher paper and lay your coloring sheet where you would like it on your shirt with the design facing down.

Note: You may want to use heat resistant tape to hold it in place.

Lay your butcher paper back on top of the T-shirt and then press using your EasyPress for 40 seconds. Use firm, steady pressure and

be careful not to slide the EasyPress or move your hands around while it's being pressed. At the end of the 40 seconds, carefully lift the EasyPress and leave your shirt with the butcher paper on top of the design to cool.

Once your design has cooled, lift the butcher paper and carefully peel up the laser copy paper, revealing your design!

Next, lay your picture frame color-side down on your shirt, framing your monster family. You may want to use heat-safe tape to hold it in place. Place the butcher paper back on top of the T-shirt and then press using your EasyPress for 40 seconds. Use firm, steady pressure and be careful not to slide the EasyPress or move your hands around while it's being pressed. At the end of the 40 seconds, carefully lift the EasyPress and leave your shirt with the butcher paper on top of the design to cool.

Step 6.

Step 6.

Note: If the transfer sheet doesn't come up with the plastic backer, use a pair of tweezers to carefully lift it up.

Machine wash in cold water inside out with mild detergent. Tumble dry low or line dry. Do not use fabric softener, dryer sheets, or bleach.

And there you have it! An adorable monster family! Create your own drawings on your iPad, export them as PNGs, and make your own coloring sheets and Infusible Ink projects using your Cricut cutting machine!

INFUSIBLE INK "MERMAID VIBES ONLY" BEACH TOTE

Cricut Explore **or** Cricut Maker Project (Cricut Joy Compatible)

Can a crafter ever have too many tote bags? I think not! From shopping for produce at the farmers' market, to holding gear for the beach, to hauling craft supplies for a crafternoon with friends—tote bags have so many great uses! Cricut Infusible Ink tote bags come in two sizes: 14 x 14 inches and 19 x 14 inches. For this project, I decided to infuse some serious beach vibes into my tote bag, and there's nothing more beachy than a mermaid. Cricut's Mermaid Rainbow Infusible Ink Transfer Sheets make creating a beautiful mermaid tail so simple! What other designs can you put on a tote bag? Add a quote from your favorite book to a bag you can take to the library or bookstore. Create a design that captures your favorite sport or hobby. Once you experience putting Infusible Ink on a tote bag, you'll be hooked!

Materials:

- Mermaid Vibes cut file
- Infusible Ink Tote
- Measuring tape
- Regular grip cutting mat
- Fine-tip blade
- Cricut Mermaid Infusible Ink Transfer Sheet for mermaid tail
- Cricut Infusible Ink Transfer Sheet in your desired color or pattern for words
- Weeding tools
- Cricut EasyPress Mat
- Cardstock
- Lint roller
- Butcher paper
- Cricut EasyPress 2
- Optional: Brayer tool and heat safe tape

Directions:

Step 1: Log into Cricut Design Space and upload the Mermaid Vibes cut file using the Cut File Upload instructions on page 28 of this book.

Step 2: Measure your tote bag to determine how big you want your design to be. Size your design accordingly by clicking on the design and using either the arrow sizer in the corner, or the Size tool.

Step 2.

Step 3: Click Make It. Slide the mirror slider on each cutting mat. Lay your Infusible Ink Transfer Sheet on your cutting mat with the color facing up and liner facing down. I like rolling a brayer over the top of my transfer sheet to make sure it's really pushed down onto the cutting mat and won't shift while cutting. Choose your cutting material, load your cutting mat into your machine using the arrow button, and then click the cute little Cricut C on your machine to start cutting! When your machine is done cutting, press the arrow again to unload the mat.

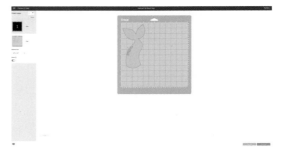

Step 3.

Step 3.

Step 4: Weed the design, removing excess transfer sheet and leaving just your design on the clear plastic backing. You will want to remove the area around the tail, the dots on the tail, the area around the letters, and then the insides of the letters, including the e, a, d, etc.

Note that the transfer sheet material is lighter than it will appear once pressed.

Step 5: Heat your Cricut EasyPress to 385°F. Place your Infusible Ink tote bag on top of your Cricut EasyPress Mat and then put a piece of cardstock inside of your tote bag to prevent the Infusible Ink from bleeding through to the back.

Use your lint roller to remove any lint, hair, or dust particles from your tote bag.

Step 5.

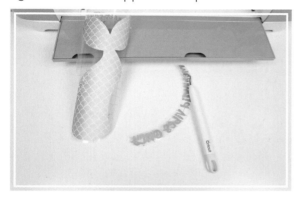

Step 4.

Lay a piece of butcher paper on top of your tote bag and heat for 15 seconds. Do not skip this step. Heating the tote bag removes any moisture from the fabric and allows the Infusible Ink to properly infuse and work its magic!

Step 5 continued on next page.

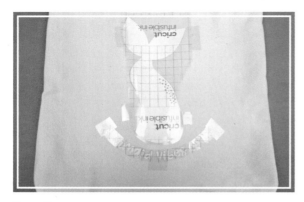

Step 5.

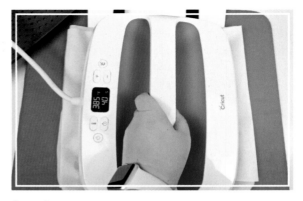

Step 5.

Remove the butcher paper and lay your design where you would like it on your tote bag.

Note: You may want to use heat-safe tape to hold it in place.

Lay your butcher paper back on top of the tote bag and then press using your EasyPress for 40 seconds. Use firm, steady pressure and be careful to not slide the EasyPress or move your hands around while it's being pressed. You want your EasyPress to remain still with firm pressure. At the end of the 40 seconds carefully lift the EasyPress and leave your tote bag with the butcher paper on top of the design to cool.

Once your design has cooled, lift the butcher paper and carefully peel up the plastic liner, revealing your design!

Note: If the transfer sheet doesn't come up with the plastic backer, use a pair of tweezers to carefully lift it up.

Machine wash in cold water inside out with mild detergent. Tumble dry low or line dry. Do not use fabric softener, dryer sheets, or bleach.

Fill your tote bag with your favorite gear for a day at the beach, or use whenever you need some mermaid vibes in your life!

INFUSIBLE INK FOOD & DRINK COASTERS

Cricut Explore **or** Cricut Maker Project (Cricut Joy Compatible)

Let's end our Infusible Ink journey with another coaster project! With our succulent coasters, we used Cricut's round ceramic Infusible Ink coasters combined with Infusible Ink pens. In this project, we are using Cricut's cork-backed square Infusible Ink coasters combined with Infusible Ink Rainbow Transfer Sheets. I love how bright and colorful these coasters are, combined with the simple font. I had so much fun coming up with the sayings for each design! Have an idea for another saying you'd love to have on a coaster? Design your own in Cricut Design Space! The Kyden font is available with a Cricut Access subscription and is very similar to the font that I used in this project.

Materials:

- Food & Drink Coaster cut files
- Regular grip cutting mat
- Fine-tip blade
- Cricut Rainbow Infusible Ink Transfer Sheet
- Cricut EasyPress Mat
- Cardstock
- Infusible Ink cork-backed square coaster blanks
- Lint roller or lint-free cloth
- Butcher paper
- Cricut EasyPress 2

Directions:

Step 1: Log into Cricut Design Space and upload the Food & Drink Cut File Upload instructions from page 28 of this book.

Step 2: Size each coaster cut file to 4 x 4 inches by clicking on each coaster design and using either the arrow sizer in the corner, or the Size box in the upper toolbar. (Cricut's square coasters measure 3.75 x 3.75 inches. Sizing your designs 4 x 4 inches will leave some border around each coaster so that you can make sure it's completely covered with infusible ink.)

Step 2.

Step 3: Click Make It. Slide the mirror slider on the cutting mat. Position your coasters where you would like them on your cutting mat. I chose to scatter my coasters across the transfer sheet so that I would get different rainbow color combinations on each coaster. Lay your Infusible Ink transfer sheet on your cutting mat with the color facing up and liner facing down. I like rolling a brayer over the top of my transfer sheet to make sure it's really pushed down onto the cutting mat and won't shift while cutting. Choose your cutting material, load your cutting mat into your machine using the arrow button, and then click the cute little Cricut C on your machine to start cutting! When your machine is done cutting, press the arrow again to unload the mat.

Weed the coaster designs, removing the Infusible Ink from around each coaster and the letters from within. Make sure to leave the centers of the letters, including the a, p, r, etc. Cut around each coaster so that it is by itself on a piece of plastic backing.

Step 3.

Step 3.

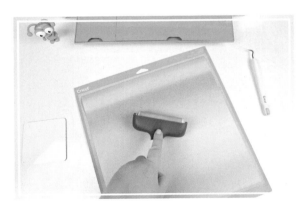

Step 3.

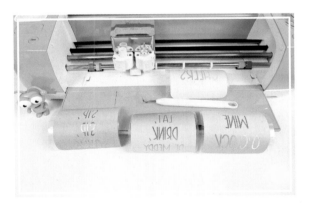

Step 3.

Step 4: Set the temperature of your Cricut EasyPress 2 to 400°F and the timer to 240 seconds. Lay out your EasyPress Mat and cover it with a piece of cardstock.

Set your coaster on your EasyPress Mat with the shiny side facing up. Use a lint roller or a lint-free cloth to wipe any dust or lint from your coaster. Don't skip this step; it's an important one to make sure your design infuses into the coaster properly.

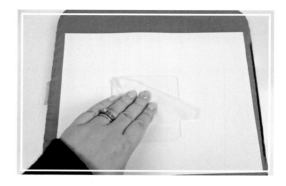

Lay your design onto the cardstock with the color side facing up. Position your coaster on top of the design with the white side facing down. Cover with a piece of butcher paper. Press using your Cricut EasyPress 2. Do not move the EasyPress around. Keep it as still as possible and apply firm, steady pressure.

When your EasyPress beeps that the timer is done, carefully lift your EasyPress, making sure not to disrupt the coaster. Your coaster is going to be VERY HOT, so don't touch it. Leave to allow your ink to finish infusing until your coaster is cool to the touch.

Once the coaster is cool, lift it up, separating the coaster from the design.

And there you have it! Infusible Ink coasters really are so much fun! They make great housewarming gifts, and between using Infusible Ink Transfer Sheets and Infusible Ink pens, the possibilities really are endless! Make sure you check out our Succulent Coasters on page 217 of this book to learn how to use Infusible Ink Pens on coasters!

An Introduction to Special Materials

We've covered seven of the most popular Cricut craft materials—but, really, that's just the tip of the crafting iceberg. You can do so many other things with your Cricut!

In this section, we're going to engrave metal, etch glass, give our cell phones a pretty makeover, take a "trip down under" with a fun felt project, blast to the crafting past with some fun shrink plastic zipper pulls, and finally learn how to use the We R Memory Keepers Foil Quill!

I hope the projects in this section, as well as the rest of the book, inspire you to create amazing things and think outside the box when it comes to crafting!

ℰNGRAVED ℚUOTE ℬRACELET

Cricut Maker Project

Need one more reason to join the Cricut Maker family? It engraves! Yep, you read that right! **It engraves!** Cricut created an engraving tip that can be used in the Adaptive Tool slot of the Cricut Maker! Head to your local craft store, check out the jewelry section, and you'll be amazed by all of the incredible blanks you can engrave on—dog tags, pendants, bracelets, earrings, and more! I'm going to show you how to make a beautiful engraved quote bracelet in this project! Pick a quote, names, dates, or any words that are significant to you and get engraving. Use these exact same steps for engraving any blanks you find in the jewelry section of your favorite craft store!

Materials:

- Bracelet blank (the ones I use are from ImpressArt)
- StrongGrip cutting mat
- Masking tape or painter's tape
- Cricut Engraving Tip
- Bracelet bending bar
- Optional: Metal stamp enamel marker and soft cloth

Directions:

Step 1: Log into Cricut Design Space. Use the Text tool and type the words you want engraved on your bracelet. Change the Linetype to Engrave. Select the font you want to use. I like filtering by fonts in a handwriting style.

Step 1.

Step 1.

Step 2: Measure your blank bracelet and determine how tall your font can be. Size your word to the appropriate size for your bracelet using the arrow buttons that appear in the corner when you click on the words or the Size tool in the toolbar. Once your word is sized correctly, click on the design and look for the + sign that shows where the center of your design is. Make note of where the center of your design is. You will use it when positioning your bracelet on your cutting mat.

Step 2.

Step 3: Click Make It. Place your bracelet on the cutting mat and tape it into place. I like to put my bracelet so it's centered on one of the lines. Pay careful attention to where the bracelet is on the cutting mat, then in Design Space, place your word so that it's centered where your bracelet is on the cutting mat. Click Continue and connect your Cricut Maker. Select Aluminum Sheet as your cutting material.

Load your Cricut Maker with your engraving tip. Use the arrow button on your machine to load your mat, then press the flashing Cricut C.

When your Cricut is done engraving, press the arrow button again to unload your mat.

Step 3.

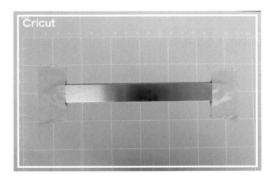

Step 3.

Step 3.

Step 3.

Step 4: Use your bracelet bending bar to bend your bracelet.

Optional step: If you want your engraved lines to be darker, use a metal stamp enamel marker to color over the letters. Leave the paint on for 2 minutes and then wipe away with a clean, dry cloth.

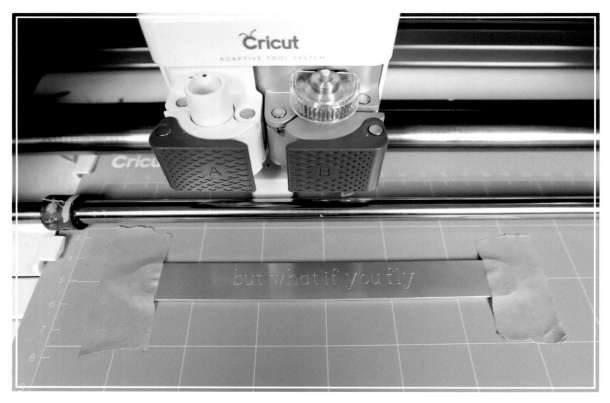

Step 4.

I think this project is one of the most unexpected things you can do with your Cricut. I love how fast and easy it is to make. It takes fewer than 10 minutes to design and engrave a beautiful bracelet! Think of other things you can engrave: a necklace with the names and birthdates of children, pet tags, zipper pulls, keychains, and more! Share your Cricut Maker engraved project on Instagram and use the hashtag #hcfcricutcrafts and tag @hellocreativefamily.

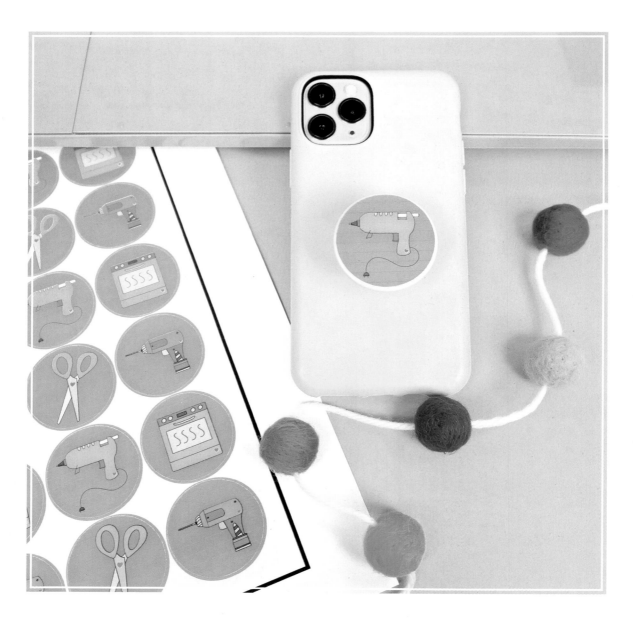

CRAFT TOOL POPSOCKET COVERS

Cricut Explore **or** Cricut Maker Project

By the time you reach this point in the book, it shouldn't come as a big surprise that I love everything handmade. Even when I buy things at the store, I love adding my own personalized, DIY touch to it. Case in point: my iPhone case. Cell phone cases are so fun to customize to fit your personality! You could cover your whole cell phone case with a fun design, or keep it simple and cover the pop socket with a fun sticker you can easily change whenever the mood strikes! Since I love crafts so much—and I'm guessing you must be a crafty person, too—for this project I'm sharing Craft Tool Popsocket Covers! I created these cute craft tool designs for my last book, *Caticorn Crafts*. We used the tools as safety icons throughout the book. I love them so much that I thought we would repurpose the designs to help decorate all our crafty cell phones! Once you know the basics of this project, you can create your own popsocket covers using your own designs and Cricut's Print and Cut function!

Materials:

- Craft Tool Popsocket cut file
- Printable vinyl or printable sticker paper
- Printer
- Regular grip cutting mat
- Fine-tip blade
- Cell phone with a popsocket

Directions:

Step 1: Log into Cricut Design Space. Upload the Craft Tools Popsocket Covers using the Cut File Upload instructions from page 28 of this book for uploading Print and Cut designs.

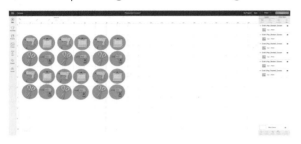

Step 1.

Step 2: Measure your popsocket to determine how big your stickers need to be. My popsocket is 1.5 inches across, so I want my stickers to be just shy of 1.5 inches each. Click on the image and use the sizing arrows and the Design Space measurement grid to get your stickers to the correct size.

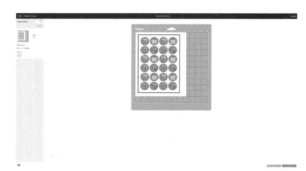

Step 2.

Step 3: Click Make It. Print your popsocket covers using your printer. Set your material type to printable vinyl or printable stickers, depending on what material you are using. Lay your printed page on your cutting mat and load it into your Cricut using the arrow button on your machine. Press the flashing C.

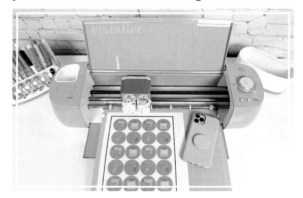

Step 3.

Step 4: Once your Cricut has cut the stickers, remove the sheet from the cutting mat, peel up a sticker, and place it on your popsocket.

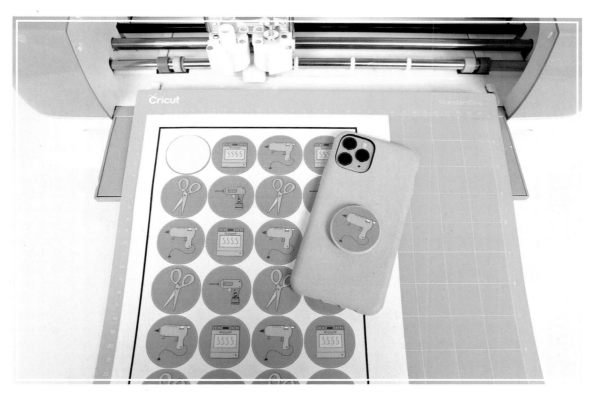

Step 4.

Cricut's Print and Cut function is so much fun to use! What other projects can you think up using printable vinyl and the Print and Cut function?

Sippin' Pretty Etched Glass Wine Glasses

Cricut Explore **or** Cricut Maker Project (Cricut Joy Compatible)

Before I got my first Cricut cutting machine, I heard a rumor that the Cricut could etch glass! *What is this magic?* I thought to myself. Well, the truth is that the Cricut itself doesn't etch the glass; however, you can definitely create beautiful etched glass work with a little help from your Cricut. The secret is stencil vinyl and etching cream! For this wine glass, I decided to create a frosted heart with the words *sippin' pretty* in the negative space within the heart. I love the idea of creating a whole collection of wine glasses with different sayings on them (you could use the Food & Drink Coasters on page 241 of this book for a bit of inspiration!). Having different sayings on each of your glasses helps your guests keep track of their glasses. Once you know how to create etched glass using your Cricut, there are so many possibilities of what you can make. Everywhere you look, you'll see a glass surface that's just waiting to have a design etched in it! Make sure you share your designs with me on Instagram by using the hashtag **#hcfcricutcrafts** and tagging **@hellocreativefamily!**

Materials:
- Wine glass
- Dish soap
- Rubbing alcohol
- Measuring tape
- Sippin' Pretty cut file
- Stencil vinyl (in a pinch, you can also use regular vinyl)
- Regular grip cutting mat
- Fine-tip blade
- Weeding tools
- Transfer tape
- Scraper tool
- Rubber gloves
- Etching cream
- Paint brush

Directions:

Step 1: Clean your wine glass well using soap and water. Then wipe off with rubbing alcohol.

Step 2: Log into Cricut Design Space. Upload the Sippin' Pretty cut file using the Cut File Upload instructions from page 28 of this book. Measure the section of your wine glass that you want your etched glass to cover and size your design accordingly by either clicking on the design and using the arrow button in the right-hand corner or by using the **Size** tool in the upper toolbar.

Step 2.

Step 3: With both pieces of your design selected, click **Attach** in the bottom right-hand toolbar. Click **Make It**. Follow the prompts on the screen, selecting Stencil Vinyl as your cutting material. Lay your stencil vinyl on your cutting mat with the paper backing facing down and load it into your Cricut using the arrow button on your machine. Press the flashing C. When your Cricut is done cutting, press the arrow to unload your cutting mat.

Step 3.

Step 4: Use your weeding tool to weed your vinyl, removing the area around the square and inside the heart, leaving the letters and square behind on the white paper backing. Don't forget to weed the center of the letters, including the inside of the p, e, y, etc.

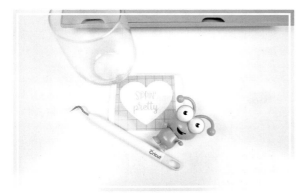

Step 4.

Step 5: Cut a piece of transfer tape slightly larger than your design. Peel off the paper backing and lay the transfer tape over your weeded design. Run your scraper tool over the transfer tape, pushing the tape down onto your vinyl. Carefully peel up the transfer tape, making sure each piece of your design lifts with the transfer tape.

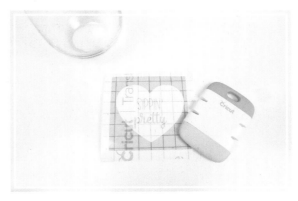

Step 5.

Pro-Crafter Tip
It can be challenging to get a design to lay flat on a curved surface. I like to use my scissors to cut slits around the transfer tape to help the tape curve better. For this design, you can cut into the square surrounding the heart, as well. Just make sure you don't cut into the heart.

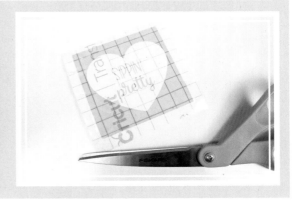

Step 6: Lay your transfer tape where you would like your design on the glass. Use your scraper tool to push the design down onto the glass. Carefully peel up the transfer tape, leaving the stencil vinyl. Make sure that your stencil vinyl is firmly adhered to the cup. If there are any areas where the vinyl is not touching the cup, etching cream could get underneath.

Step 7: Put on rubber gloves and follow the instructions on your etching cream package. Use your paint brush to carefully dab the etching cream onto the glass, covering the area where the heart and letters are. Leave to sit for the recommended amount of time, then rinse off carefully using water.

Step 7.

Step 6.

Step 8: Remove the stencil vinyl and see your beautiful design left behind.

There are so many fun possibilities with this project from monogrammed wedding glasses, to cups for a girls' night out, to etched glass casserole dishes and pie plates!

Pro-Crafter Tip

If your glass isn't as etched as you would like it to be, carefully dry off the glass and apply more etching cream, leave on for another 5 to 10 minutes, then rinse again. I sometimes like removing the heart and then hand painting the etching cream onto the glass where the heart is to make sure my edges are nice and clean.

Shrink Plastic Donut Zipper Pull

Remember at the beginning of this book when I gave you a list of all the amazing materials that can be cut with the Cricut? Well those are just the materials that Cricut has tested cutting, but guess what? There's a way to create your own material types, cut pressure, and number of passes so that you can cut an even wider array of materials! I'm going to show you how in this super fun Donut Zipper Pull project. I grew up in the eighties when Shrinky Dinks were all the rage. It's been so much fun seeing shrink plastic become popular again now that I'm an adult crafter! I recently had the zipper on my favorite winter jacket break, so creating a zipper pull out of shrink plastic seemed like the perfect project for the time. Shrink plastic isn't listed under your Cricut's cutting materials, but these pretty pastel donuts make it worth adding!

Materials:
- Donut Zipper Pull cut file
- White printable shrink plastic
- Printer
- Regular grip cutting mat
- Fine-tip blade
- Baking sheet
- Parchment paper or aluminum foil
- Oven or toaster oven
- Jewelry pliers
- Jump rings
- Lobster clasps

Directions:

Step 1: Log into Cricut Design Space and upload the Donut Zipper Pull using the Cut File Upload instructions from page 28 of this book for uploading a Print and Cut file.

Step 2: Size your donuts so they are 3 inches wide each. You can do this by using the sizing grid, clicking on the donuts, and using the sizing arrow that appears in the bottom right-hand corner.

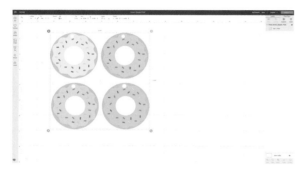

Step 2.

Step 3: Click Make It. Print your donuts on white printable shrink plastic using your printer. If using a Cricut Explore, set your dial to Custom. For both the Cricut Maker and the Cricut Explore, when it's time to select your material, click Browse Materials and then click Material Settings at the bottom of the screen. Scroll all the way to the bottom and click Add New Material. Type "Shrink Plastic" and click Continue. Set your cut pressure to 350 and your multi-cut to 2. Save your material type and then select it for this project. Load your cutting mat with the printed shrink plastic. Press the arrow button to load it into the machine then press the flashing Cricut C to start cutting. A light will appear on your Cricut and you will notice it scanning your sheet. Once it's finished detecting your borders, your machine will start cutting. When the machine has finished cutting, before unloading the mat, check to make sure the cuts have gone all the way through. If they haven't, press the Cricut C again for it to do another pass; if it has, press the arrow to unload your cutting mat.

Step 3.

Step 4: Remove your donuts from the cutting mat. Preheat your oven to the temperature recommended for the type of shrink plastic you're using. Lay your donuts on a baking tray lined with parchment paper or aluminum foil. Bake following the instructions for your shrink plastic. When donuts are done shrinking, remove them from the oven and set aside to cool.

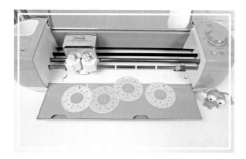

Step 4.

Step 5: Once your donuts have cooled, use your jewelry pliers to attach jump rings and a lobster clasp. Attach them to your zipper for a cute and functional accessory!

Step 5.

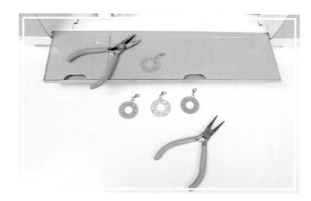

Step 5.

What other projects could you make using shrink plastic? There are so many fun projects you can make from charm bracelets, earrings, and necklaces to buttons, thumbtacks, and flare pins! Make sure to share pictures of what you make on Instagram using the hashtag #hcfcricutcrafts and tagging @hellocreativefamily!

FELT KOALA CUP COZY

I love felt. It comes in so many different colors, is readily available at the craft store, is inexpensive, and you can make so many cute things with it—like cup cozies! Caticorns, sloths, and llamas all have a special place in my animal-loving heart, but I'm predicting that koalas are going to be the next big thing. I went with a traditional color palette for my cup cozy using a classic gray for the koala, but it would also be fun to think outside the box with your colors! How cute would a lilac felt koala be? Speaking of felt, the Cricut Maker rotary blade cuts through it like butter. It's by far the easiest way to cut felt that I've ever experienced. You're going to have so much fun making this project! I would love to see your koalas in the "wild"! Share photos of your Koala Cup Cozy on Instagram and use the hashtag **#hcfcricutcrafts** and tag **@hellocreativefamily.**

Materials:

- Koala Cup Cozy cut file
- Measuring tape
- Travel mug
- 12 x 12-inch sheet gray felt
- 4 x 4-inch piece white felt
- 4 x 4-inch piece black felt
- 4 x 4-inch piece pink felt
- FabricGrip adhesive cutting mat
- Rotary blade
- Wonder clips or pins
- Sewing machine
- Thread in coordinating colors
- Scissors
- Fabric glue

Directions:

Step 1: Log into Cricut Design Space and upload the Koala Cup Cozy cut file following the Cut File Upload instructions on page 28 of this book.

Step 2: Measure the circumference of your travel mug. Divide that number in half, then add ½ inch. Click on the cut file and use the sizing grid and the arrow in the bottom right-hand corner of your design to size the gray piece at the top right of the design file to be the number you calculated above.

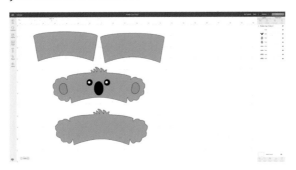

Step 2.

Step 3: Click Make It. Select Felt as your cutting material. Load your rotary blade into your Cricut Maker. Lay your first sheet of felt on your pink Cricut FabricGrip cutting mat and load it into the machine by pressing the arrow. Press the flashing Cricut C to have your machine start cutting. Once your machine has finished cutting, hit the arrow button again to eject your cutting mat. Remove the felt from the cutting mat and repeat with each color of felt.

Step 3.

Step 4: Once you have all of your Koala Cup Cozy pieces cut, set aside the eyes, nose, and inside ear pieces. You should have two cup cozy pieces that have ears and hair for the front of your cup cozy and two plain pieces for the back of your cup cozy. Take your two front pieces, line up all the edges, and pin or wonder clip into place. Take the two back pieces, line up all the edges, and pin or wonder clip into place.

Sew all the way around the outside edge of your front two pieces using a ⅛-inch seam allowance. Sew all the way around the outside edge of your back two pieces using a ⅛-inch seam allowance.

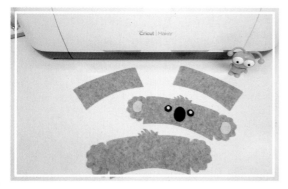

Step 4.

Step 4.

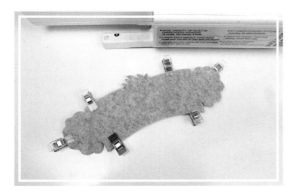

Step 4.

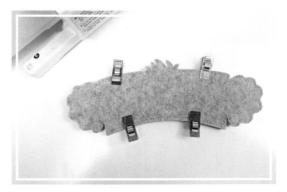

Step 4.

Step 4 continued on next page.

Once you have your two front pieces sewn together, and your two back pieces sewn together, line up the bottom edges of your front piece and back piece and pin or wonder clip in place.

Sew your front piece and your back piece together, using a ⅛-inch seam allowance. You'll want to start in the bottom corner right below the koala's ear and sew straight up to the top corner above the koalas ear. Repeat on the opposite side by the other ear.

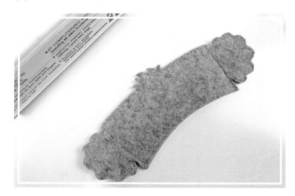

Step 4.

Step 5: Use fabric glue to sew the koala's eyes, nose, and inner ear pieces to your cup cozy. Set aside to dry for 24 hours.

Step 5.

And there you have it! An adorable Koala Cup Cozy! What other designs could you make for a cup cozy?

Let's Talk Foil Quill!

I couldn't let this book wrap up without talking a little bit about the We R Memory Keepers Foil Quill. I have an article on Hello Creative Family about how to use a Foil Quill with your Cricut and it's one of my most visited posts. People always send me Foil Quill questions. It really is an amazing little tool that is a relatively inexpensive addition to your Cricut cutting machine.

What Is a Foil Quill?

The Foil Quill allows you to turn your cutting machine into a foiling machine! The Foil Quill is a small, pen-like attachment you insert into the pen holder of your Cricut. It has a cord you plug in that heats up the tip of the Foil Quill. Lay a sheet of We R Memory Keepers foil on top of the material you would like to foil, insert it into the cutting machine, and instead of drawing your design with a pen, the Foil Quill will draw it with foil!

What Tip Sizes Does the Foil Quill Come In?

The Foil Quill currently comes in three tip sizes: fine, standard, and bold. I have a standard tip Foil Quill.

What Materials Can You Foil?

The Foil Quill is a dream come true for card-makers and other paper crafters; however, you can use it on other materials, too! Some of my favorite materials to foil are cardstock, faux leather, felt, and chipboard!

Other materials that We R Memory Keepers says you can foil on are:

- Book board
- Vinyl
- Acetate
- Vellum
- Leather
- Fabric
- Wood

A Special Note about the Foil Quill

The Foil Quill is not made by Cricut, nor endorsed by Cricut. Since it's a third-party attachment that Cricut has not tested itself, using a Foil Quill in your machine could void your warranty. We R Memory Keepers has a note on their website saying to contact them if you run into any warranty issues with your Cricut as a result of the Foil Quill.

Foil Quill Faux Leather Lip Balm Holder

Cricut Explore or Cricut Maker Project

My sister and I have a "thing" for lip balm. We love the stuff and have them stashed in all kinds of secret places for whenever a lip balm emergency should present itself. My sister loves her lip balm so much that her son's first word was "Chapstick"! While I've had some mixed experiences with using my Foil Quill with leather (if the leather is too smooth, I find the foil doesn't adhere well), I've always had success foil quilling faux leather. I've tested my Foil Quill with multiple finishes of faux leather, from pebbled to wood grain to suede, and each time I've gotten great coverage and fabulous adhesion. For this project, we're making a faux leather lip balm holder that you can Foil Quill with a cute saying, your name, initials, or even a design. I chose to go with the saying *Pucker up*. These lip balm holders would make great stocking stuffers and Valentine's Day gifts. Attach it to your keys, purse, or backpack and your lip balm will always be within reach! What saying will you put on yours?

Materials:

- We R Memory Keepers Foil Quill
- Lip Balm Holder cut file
- Regular grip cutting mat
- Faux leather
- We R Memory Keepers Foil Sheet
- Washi tape
- Fine-tip blade
- Key ring or carabiner
- Pins or wonder clips
- Sewing machine
- Thread in coordinating colors
- Scissors

Directions:

Step 1: The We R Memory Keepers Foil Quill needs to preheat for 5 minutes before use. The Foil Quill comes with adaptors for four different types of machines. The first thing you'll want to do is to select the adaptor that works with the Cricut. It is marked with a C. Slide it onto the Foil Quill and tighten it until it's fingertip tight.

Next, you'll want to pop the pen adaptor out of your Cricut. Your pen adaptor comes installed inside your Cricut and you may not even know it's there! To remove it, reach underneath the pen holder and press up firmly but gently. The adaptor will pop up and you can pull it out. Now that your pen holder is empty, you can insert your Foil Quill tool. Insert it into the holder and then close the Cricut clamp to lock it in place.

Next, you want to plug in your Foil Quill. The cord isn't super long so you'll probably want to have an extension cord pretty close with a USB adaptor plugin. You can also plug it into your laptop, or if you're using a Cricut Maker, the USB adaptor on the side of the machine. Once it's plugged in, a light will appear on your Foil Quill. The Foil Quill comes with a metal protective plate. Insert this under the tip of your Foil Quill and let your Foil Quill heat up for 5 minutes.

Step 1.

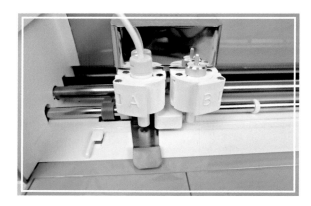

Step 1.

Step 2: While your Foil Quill is heating, log into Cricut Design Space and upload the Lip Balm Holder cut file following the Cut File Upload instructions on page 28 of this book.

Step 3: For standard-sized lip balm, size your cut file so that it is 8 inches tall. Do this by clicking on the design and using either the arrow button on the bottom right-hand corner or the **Size** tool in the top toolbar.

Step 4: Now it's time to decide what you would like foiled on your lip balm holder. Once you decide on the text, click on the text box on the left-hand side of your screen. Type in what you would like foiled, and then click on the **Font** box. I then click on the **Filter** button and select a font that is single layer and is in handwriting style. Once you have selected your font and typed the words you would like foiled, change your linetype to **Draw** in the upper toolbar.

For my project, I used the Kyden font and changed my letter space to 2 and my line space to 2.5. I also added a heart from the shape menu and changed the **Linetype** to **Draw**.

Step 4.

Step 5: Position your text where you would like it on the small rectangle piece of your lip balm holder. You may want to use the **Center** button under the **Alignment** tool. Once you have your text where you would like it, select both the rectangle and the text and click **Attach**. This will make your Foil Quill draw your design where you want it on the rectangle piece.

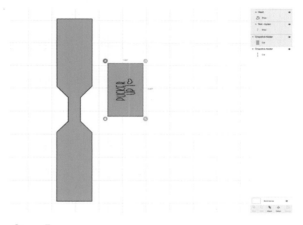

Step 5.

Step 6: Click Make It. Lay your faux leather on top of your cutting mat and smooth it down firmly. Take a piece of We R Memory Keepers Foil and lay it on your cutting mat where your machine will be foiling. Tape it in place using washi tape. Connect your Cricut to Design Space and select the type of material you're cutting. Remove the metal protective plate from under your Foil Quill and load your cutting mat into the Cricut by pressing the arrow button. Press the flashing C and your machine will start foiling. When the foiling has finished, press the pause button, remove the foil from your project, and press the pause button again, and your machine will start cutting. When your machine is done cutting, press the arrow button to unload your mat.

Step 6.

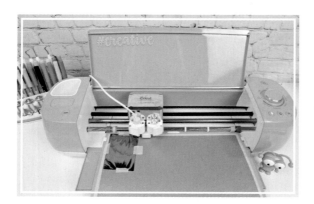

Step 6.

Step 7: Remove your cut pieces of faux leather from your cutting mat. Slip your key ring over your large piece of the lip balm holder. Fold the piece in half so all your edges are lined up and the key ring is resting in the thin loop. Line the rectangular piece of your faux leather up with the large piece, at the opposite end from where your key ring is. With all the pieces lined up, wonder clip or pin in place.

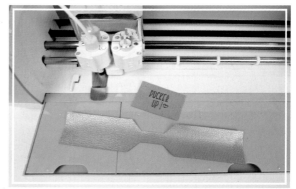

Step 7.

Step 8: Use your sewing machine to sew all the way around the edges of your lip balm holder using a ⅛-inch seam allowance. When you get to the loop area, sew straight across the bottom of the loop and then continue sewing along the edge of the faux leather. Don't forget to backstitch at the beginning and end. Use your scissors to trim your excess thread.

Step 8.

Stick your favorite lip balm in the pocket of your lip balm holder and never be caught with chapped lips! There are so many possibilities for this fun project from all of the different designs you could foil on it, to different types of materials you could use, like felt. I'd love to see what you come up with! Share your project on Instagram and use the hashtag #hcfcricutcrafts and tag @hellocreativefamily!

And now we've come to the end of the book!

I sure did have fun Cricuting with you! I hope that the projects in this book gave you the confidence to try cutting some materials you've never tried cutting with your Cricut before. I also hope that the projects act as a launch pad and inspire you to create some brand new projects based on these designs.

I would love to hear from you! Please be in touch with any thoughts, questions, and success stories! I would love to see photos of your finished projects. You can find me anytime at hellocreativefamily.com and by email at crystal@hellocreativefamily.com.

Happy crafting, friends!

APPENDIX:
Which Materials Can Each Cricut Cut?

Cricut Joy Cutting Materials:

Corrugated Cardboard
Flat Cardboard
Foil Poster Board
Glitter Cardstock
Insert Card—Cardstock
Medium Cardstock—80 lb
   (216 gsm)
Everyday Iron-On Mesh
Everyday Iron-On Mosaic
Glitter Mesh Iron-On
Holographic Iron-On
Holographic Iron-On Mosaic
Holographic Sparkle Iron-On
Infusible Ink Transfer Sheet
Smart Iron-On
Smart Iron-On—Glitter
Smart Iron-On—Holographic
Smart Iron-On—Patterned
SportFlex Iron-On
Faux Leather (Paper Thin)
Deluxe Paper
Deluxe Paper, Adhesive
   Backed

Deluxe Paper Foil Embossed
Foil Paper—0.36mm
Pearl Paper
Shimmer Paper
Smart Label Writable Paper
Sparkle Paper
True Brushed Paper
Foil Acetate
Adhesive Foil
Chalkboard Vinyl
Dry Erase Vinyl
Holographic Sparkle Vinyl
Premium Vinyl
Premium Vinyl—Frosted
   Glitter
Premium Vinyl—Frosted Gray
Premium Vinyl—Frosted
   Opaque
Premium Vinyl—Holographic
Premium Vinyl—Holographic
   3D Textured
Premium Vinyl—Holographic
   Art Deco

Cricut Explore Cutting Materials

The Cricut Explore Air 2 has a smart set dial on it that allows you to cut these materials with the turn of a knob. Here are the materials that the Cricut Explore Air 2 can cut, all using fine-point blades.

Paper -
Paper
Paper +
Vinyl
Vinyl +

Iron-On
Iron-On +
Light Cardstock
Light Cardstock +
Cardstock

Cardstock +
Fabric*
Fabric +*
Poster Board
Poster Board +

Turn the smart set dial on your Cricut Explore Air 2 to **CUSTOM** and you can cut these additional materials. Use a fine-point blade unless otherwise specified.

Adhesive Foil
Adhesive Foil, Matte
Aluminum—0.14mm
Aluminum Foil Deep-Point
   Blade
Birch
Burlap, Bonded* (Bonded
   Fabric Blade)
Canvas
Cardstock (for intricate cuts)
Chalkboard Vinyl
Clear Printable Sticker Paper
Construction Paper
Copy Paper—20 lb
Cork, Adhesive-Backed
Corrugated Cardboard
Craft Foam (Deep-Point
   Blade)
Cutting Mat Protector

Deluxe Paper
Deluxe Paper Foil, Embossed
Denim, Bonded* (Bonded
   Fabric Blade)
Distressed Craft Foam (Deep-
   Point Blade)
Duct Tape Sheet
Embossed Foil Paper
Epoxy Glitter Paper
Everyday Iron-On
Everyday Iron-On Mesh
Faux Leather (Paper Thin)
Faux Suede
Felt
Felt, Wool Bonded*
Felt, Wool Fabric
Flat Cardboard
Flocked Paper
Foil Acetate

Foil Iron-On
 Foil Paper—0.36mm
Foil Poster Board
Fusible Fabric
Genuine Leather (Deep-Point
   Blade)
Glitter Cardstock
Glitter Iron-On
Glitter Mesh Iron-On
Glitter Vinyl
Grocery Bag
Heavy Patterned Paper
Heavy Watercolor
   Paper—140 lb
Holographic Iron-On
Holographic Poster Board
Holographic Sparkle Iron-On
Holographic Sparkle Vinyl
Kraft Board

Kraft Cardstock
Light Chipboard—0.37mm
Light Chipboard—0.55mm
Light Glitter Paper
Light Patterned Paper
Magnetic Sheet—0.5mm
Magnetic Sheet—0.6mm
(Deep-Point Blade)
Magnetic Sheet, Adhesive
Backed—0.35mm
Medium Cardstock—80 lb
Metallic Leather (Deep-Point
Blade)
Metallic Poster Board
Neon Iron-On
Non-Adhesive Vinyl—16
gauge
Notebook Paper
Oil Cloth, Bonded* (Bonded
Fabric Blade)
Paint Chip
Parchment Paper
Party Foil

Patterned Iron-On
Pearl Paper
Photo Paper
Plush Craft Foam (Deep-Point
Blade)
Polyester, Bonded* (Bonded
Fabric Blade)
Poster Board
Premium Outdoor Vinyl
Premium Vinyl
Premium Vinyl-Frosted Glitter
Premium Vinyl-Frosted Gray
Premium Vinyl-Frosted
Opaque
Premium Vinyl-Holographic
Premium Vinyl-Pearl
Premium Vinyl-Shimmer
Premium Vinyl-Textured
Premium Vinyl-Textured,
Metallic
Premium Vinyl-True Brushed
Printable Fabric
Printable Iron-On, Dark

Printable Iron-On, Light
Printable Vinyl
Shimmer Leather—1mm
Shimmer Paper
Silk, Bonded* (Bonded Fabric
Blade)
Sparkle Paper
SportFlex Iron-On
Stencil Film—0.4mm
Stencil Vinyl
Sticker Paper
Sticky Note
Tattoo Paper
Transparency
True Brushed Paper
Vellum
Washi Sheet
Washi Tape—0.06mm
Wax Paper
Window Cling

Wrapping Paper

Cricut Maker Cutting Materials:

The Cricut Maker doesn't have a smart set dial. Instead, you select your cutting material from a material list within Cricut Design Space. Here are the 300+ materials the Cricut Maker can cut and the blade type that you use to cut them. Please be aware that more materials are added to Cricut's list of cutting materials as new Adaptive Tools are released.

2–3 oz. Garment Leather (0.8 mm) | Knife Blade

2–3 oz. Tooling Leather (0.8 mm) | Rotary Blade

4–5 oz. Garment Leather (1.6 mm) | Knife Blade

4–5 oz. Tooling Leather (1.6 mm) | Knife Blade

6–7 oz. Tooling Leather (2.4 mm) | Knife Blade

Acetate | Fine-Point Blade

Adhesive Foil | Fine-Point Blade

Adhesive Foil, Matte | Fine-Point Blade

Adhesive Sheet, Double-Sided | Fine-Point Blade

Aluminum Foil Deep-Point Blade

Balsa—1/16" (1.6 mm) | Knife Blade

Balsa—3/32" (2.4 mm) | Knife Blade

Bamboo Fabric | Rotary Blade

Basswood—1/16" (1.6 mm) | Knife Blade

Basswood—1/32" (0.8 mm) | Knife Blade

Bengaline | Rotary Blade

Birch, Permanent Adhesive | Fine-Point Blade

Boucle | Rotary Blade

Broadcloth | Rotary Blade

Burlap | Rotary Blade

Burn-Out Velvet | Rotary Blade

Calico | Rotary Blade

Cambric | Rotary Blade

Canvas | Rotary Blade

Carbon Fiber | Fine-Point Blade

Cardstock (for intricate cuts) | Fine-Point Blade

Cardstock, Adhesive-Backed | Fine-Point Blade

Cashmere | Rotary Blade

Cereal Box| Deep-Point Blade

Chalkboard Vinyl | Fine-Point Blade

Challis | Rotary Blade

Chambray | Rotary Blade

Chantilly Lace | Rotary Blade

Charmeuse Satin | Rotary Blade

Damask Chipboard | Knife Blade

Delicate Fabrics (like Tulle) | Rotary Blade

Delicate Fabrics (like Tulle), Bonded | Bonded Fabric Blade

Deluxe Paper | Fine-Point Blade

Denim | Rotary Blade

Denim, Bonded | Bonded Fabric Blade

Dotted Swiss | Rotary Blade

Double Cloth | Rotary Blade

Double Knit | Rotary Blade

Dry Erase Vinyl | Fine-Point Blade

Duck Cloth | Rotary Blade

Duct Tape Sheet | Fine-Point Blade

Dupioni Silk | Rotary Blade

EVA Foam | Deep-Point Blade

Everyday Iron-On | Fine-Point Blade

Everyday Iron-On Mesh | Fine-Point Blade

Extra Heavy Fabrics (like Burlap) | Rotary Blade

Eyelet | Rotary Blade

Faille | Rotary Blade

Faux Fur | Rotary Blade

Faux Leather (Paper Thin) | Fine-Point Blade

Faux Suede | Fine-Point Blade

Faux Suede | Rotary Blade

Felt | Fine-Point Blade

Felt, Acrylic Fabric | Rotary Blade

Felt, Craft Bonded | Bonded Fabric Blade

Felt, Glitter Bonded | Rotary Blade

Felt, Stiff | Fine-Point Blade

Felt, Wool Bonded | Fine-Point Blade

Felt, Wool Fabric | Rotary Blade

Flannel | Rotary Blade

Flat Cardboard | Fine-Point Blade

Fleece | Rotary Blade

Flex Foam | Rotary Blade

Flocked Iron-On | Fine-Point Blade

Flocked Paper | Fine-Point Blade

Foil Acetate | Fine-Point Blade

Foil Iron-On | Fine-Point Blade

Foil Paper—0.36mm | Fine-Point Blade

Foil Poster Board | Fine-Point Blade

Foulard | Rotary Blade

Freezer Paper | Fine-Point Blade

Fusible Fabric | Rotary Blade

Fusible Fleece | Rotary Blade

Fusible Interfacing | Rotary Blade

Gabardine | Rotary Blade

Gauze | Rotary Blade

Gel Sheet | Deep-Point Blade

Genuine Leather | Deep-Point Blade

Georgette | Rotary Blade

Glitter Cardstock | Fine-Point Blade

Glitter Craft Foam | Fine-Point Blade

Glitter Duct Tape | Fine-Point Blade

Glitter Iron-On | Fine-Point Blade

Glitter Mesh Iron-On | Fine-Point Blade

Glitter Vinyl | Fine-Point Blade

Gossamer | Rotary Blade

Grocery Bag | Fine-Point Blade

Grois Point | Rotary Blade

Grosgrain | Rotary Blade

Habutai | Rotary Blade

Handmade Paper | Rotary Blade

Heat Transfer (non-Cricut) | Fine-Point Blade

Heather | Rotary Blade

Heavy Chipboard—2.0mm | Knife Blade

Heavy Fabrics (like Denim) | Rotary Blade

Heavy Fabrics (like Denim), Bonded | Bonded Fabric Blade

Heavy Patterned Paper | Fine-Point Blade

Heavy Watercolor Paper—140 lb (300 gsm) | Fine-Point Blade

Holographic Cardstock | Fine-Point Blade

Holographic Heat Transfer | Fine-Point Blade

Holographic Iron-On | Fine-Point Blade

Holographic Sparkle Iron-On | Fine-Point Blade

Holographic Sparkle Vinyl | Fine-Point Blade

Homespun Fabric | Rotary Blade

Insulbrite Batting | Rotary Blade

Interlock Knit | Rotary Blade

Iron-On | Fine-Point Blade

Jacquard | Rotary Blade

Jersey | Rotary Blade

Jute | Rotary Blade

Kevlar | Rotary Blade

Khaki | Rotary Blade

Kraft Board | Fine-Point Blade

Kraft Cardstock | Fine-Point Blade

La Coste | Rotary Blade

Lame | Rotary Blade

Light Cardstock—60 lb (163 gsm) | Fine-Point Blade

Light Chipboard—0.37mm | Fine-Point Blade

Light Cotton | Rotary Blade

Light Cotton, 2 layers Rotary Blade

Light Cotton, 3 layers Rotary Blade

Light Fabrics (like Silk) | Rotary Blade

Light Fabrics (like Silk), Bonded | Bonded Fabric Blade

Light Patterned Paper | Fine-Point Blade

Linen | Rotary Blade

Linen, Bonded Bonded Fabric Blade

Lycra | Rotary Blade

Magnetic Sheet—0.5mm | Fine-Point Blade

Magnetic Sheet—0.6mm | Deep-Point Blade

Matboard 4 Ply | Knife Blade

Matelasse | Rotary Blade

Matte Vinyl | Fine-Point Blade

Medium Cardstock—80 lb (216 gsm) | Fine-Point Blade

Medium Fabrics (like Cotton) | Rotary Blade

Medium Fabrics (like Cotton), Bonded

Bonded Fabric Blade

Melton Wool | Rotary Blade

Mesh | Rotary Blade

Metal—40 gauge thin copper | Fine-Point Blade

Metallic Leather | Deep-Point Blade

Metallic Poster Board | Fine-Point Blade

Metallic Vinyl | Fine-Point Blade

Microfiber | Rotary Blade

Moiree | Rotary Blade

Moleskin | Rotary Blade

Monk's Cloth | Rotary Blade

Mulberry Paper | Rotary Blade

Muslin | Rotary Blade

Neoprene | Deep-Point Blade

Non-Adhesive Vinyl—16 gauge | Fine-Point Blade

Non-Adhesive Vinyl—20 gauge | Fine-Point Blade

Notebook Paper | Fine-Point Blade

Nylon | Rotary Blade

Oilcloth, Bonded | Bonded Fabric Blade

Oilcloth | Rotary Blade

Organza | Rotary Blade

Ottoman | Rotary Blade

Outdoor Vinyl, Bonded | Bonded Fabric Blade

Oxford | Rotary Blade
Paint Chip | Fine-Point Blade
Panne Velvet | Rotary Blade
Paper, Adhesive-Backed | Fine-Point Blade
Parchment Paper | Fine-Point Blade
Party Foil | Fine-Point Blade
Patterned Glitter Cardstock | Fine-Point Blade
Patterned Iron-On | Fine-Point Blade
Pearl Paper | Fine-Point Blade
Peau de Soie | Rotary Blade
Photo Paper | Fine-Point Blade
Pima Cotton | Rotary Blade
Pique Cotton | Rotary Blade
Plastic Canvas | Deep-Point Blade
Plastic Packaging | Fine-Point Blade
Plisse | Rotary Blade
Plush | Rotary Blade
Polyester, Bonded | Bonded Fabric Blade
Poplin | Rotary Blade
Poster Board | Fine-Point Blade
Poster Board | Fine-Point Blade
Premium Outdoor Vinyl | Fine-Point Blade

Premium Vinyl | Fine-Point Blade
Premium Vinyl—Frosted Glitter | Fine-Point Blade
Premium Vinyl—Frosted Gray | Fine-Point Blade
Premium Vinyl—Frosted Opaque | Fine-Point Blade
Premium Vinyl—Holographic | Fine-Point Blade
Premium Vinyl—Pearl | Fine-Point Blade
Premium Vinyl—Shimmer | Fine-Point Blade
Premium Vinyl—Textured | Fine-Point Blade
Premium Vinyl—Textured Metallic | Fine-Point Blade
Premium Vinyl—True Brushed | Fine-Point Blade
Printable Fabric | Fine-Point Blade
Printable Foil | Fine-Point Blade
Printable Iron-On, Dark | Fine-Point Blade
Printable Iron-On, Light | Fine-Point Blade
Printable Magnetic Sheet | Fine-Point Blade
Printable Vinyl | Fine-Point Blade
Quilt Batting | Rotary Blade

Ramie | Rotary Blade
Raschel Knit | Rotary Blade
Rayon Lyocell | Rotary Blade
Rib Knit | Rotary Blade
Rice Paper | Deep-Point Blade
Rip-Stop Nylon | Rotary Blade
Sailcloth | Rotary Blade
Sandblast Stencil | Deep-Point Blade
Satin Silk | Rotary Blade
Seersucker | Rotary Blade
Sequined | Rotary Blade
Shantung | Rotary Blade
Shantung Santeen | Rotary Blade
Shimmer Leather—1mm | Fine-Point Blade
Shimmer Paper | Fine-Point Blade
Shrinky Dink | Fine-Point Blade
Silk China | Rotary Blade
Silk, Bonded | Bonded Fabric Blade
Slinky Knit | Rotary Blade
Spandex | Rotary Blade
Sparkle Paper | Fine-Point Blade
SportFlex Iron-On | Fine-Point Blade
Stencil Film—0.4mm | Fine-Point Blade
Stencil Vinyl | Fine-Point Blade

Sticker Paper | Fine-Point Blade

Sticker Paper, Removable | Fine-Point Blade

Sticky Note | Fine-Point Blade

Suede | Rotary Blade

Tafetta | Rotary Blade

Tattoo Paper | Fine-Point Blade

Terry Cloth | Rotary Blade

Tissue Paper | Rotary Blade

Transfer Foil | Fine-Point Blade

Transfer Sheet | Fine-Point Blade

Transparency | Fine-Point Blade

True Brushed Paper | Fine-Point Blade

Tulle | Rotary Blade

Tweed | Rotary Blade

Ultra-Firm Stabilizer | Rotary Blade

Vellum | Fine-Point Blade

Velour | Rotary Blade

Velvet Upholstery | Rotary Blade

Velveteen | Rotary Blade

Vinyl | Fine-Point Blade

Viscose | Rotary Blade

Voile | Rotary Blade

Waffle Cloth | Rotary Blade

Washi Sheet | Fine-Point Blade

Wax Paper | Fine-Point Blade

Window Cling | Fine-Point Blade

Wool Crepe | Rotary Blade

Wrapping Paper | Fine-Point Blade

Ziberline | Rotary Blade

Acknowledgments

You guys! I've written two books now! How lucky am I?!?! This book would not be possible without the help, love, and support of so many people.

I want to start by saying thank you to my sister-in-law, Myra. I realized when I held a finished copy of *Caticorn Crafts* in my hands for the first time that I neglected thanking you in the acknowledgments, and I've felt awful ever since. From the day I met you (eighteen years ago!), you have been my cheerleader. You have the biggest heart of anyone that I know. You are a devoted aunt, a loving sister, and such an important member of my support system. Thank you for being such an important person in my life.

This book would not be possible without my editor, Nicole Frail. Nicole made my childhood dream of becoming an author come true when she approached me to write my first book, *Caticorn Crafts*. She made my "book dreams" come true when she asked me to write *Cricut Crafts*, a book that I had been wanting to write since the first time I used a Cricut. A good chunk of this book came together while the world was (and still is) in a very uncertain time. Nicole, I'm in awe of what a superwoman you are, juggling it all. Thank you. I love working with you and couldn't ask for a more supportive editor.

Thank you to everyone at Skyhorse Publishing for helping my books come to life and get out into the market. I know how much work it takes. Please know how much I appreciate you all.

To everyone at Cricut—thank you! Everyone that you hire has so much heart. I've never spoken to anyone at Cricut (from Ashish, the CEO of Cricut, to people on the influencer team, to members of the customer service support team) who hasn't exuded a feeling that they love what they do. You all have so much heart, and it's such a great pleasure to work with you.

A huge thank-you to my fabulous Hello Creative Family readers. You inspire me so much! Every single day, I say a thank you to all of you. It's because of your support that I get to live this creative life, which is just the most amazing gift.

To my friend and former business partner, Karen Bannister. Thank you so much for helping me come up with concept of Hello Creative Family, for helping me make the leap to rebrand, and for convincing me that leaving my day job to be my own boss would be one of the best decisions I ever made. I miss our lunchtime meetings!

To my blogger bestie Brooke from Brooklyn Berry Designs—thank you for being my sounding board to bounce ideas off of, for helping to get me back on my game on the days when I have lost my inspiration, and most importantly for being my friend!

I'm one of those lucky girls who has friends that have become family. Dunia, Heather, Karen, and Tracy—thank you for always having my back, for being my cheerleaders, and for believing in me, lifting me up, and getting me back on track when I'm filled with doubt. Love you!

To my **#TotallyFreeSVG** Crew—you gals are amazing and you inspire me so much! The first Tuesday of the month is always a happy one for me thanks to all of you. Thanks for including me in your group and for inspiring me to push myself!

Thank you to my beautiful children, Bella and Adam, for being the most wonderful things that I ever created and for being my creative inspiration.

Thank you to Mom and Dad for raising me in a creative home and for always supporting my dreams (no matter how crazy they were).

Thank you to my beautiful sister, Kara, for always being there for me and for our epic talks about life. Thank you also to her husband, Jimmy, for his generosity (and delicious farm produce) and to her two beautiful children, Jamie and Skye, for making me an aunt!

Thank you to my in-laws—Fannie, James, Myra, and Jon—for molding such a kind and loving boy who grew up to be a wonderful man, husband, and father. Thank you for your love, support, and all of your Facetime calls with the kids that keep me entertained and giggling from the sidelines.

And finally, thank you to my husband, Rob. You have been unwavering in your support and have never given me one reason to doubt that I should be doing exactly what I'm doing. You are the one and only reason that I am living my wildest dream and get to write and craft every day as a profession. Thank you. I love you.

About the Author

Crystal Allen is the owner and creative director of Hello Creative Family, a website for families looking to ignite their creativity with simple, playful, and fun crafts, DIYs, and recipes. Raised by two creative parents, Crystal is a firm believer that when kids see their parents pursuing their own creative passions they are more likely to be creative themselves-- It's that concept that is the driving force behind Hello Creative Family.

Crystal thinks that everyone has creativity within them, and it's just about finding the right creative outlet for each person— whether that's in the kitchen, craft room, garden, workshop, or in the great outdoors.

With an emphasis on projects that take sixty minutes or less to make, Hello Creative Family's goal is to inspire families everywhere to carve out a bit of time to get creative and create a handmade, homemade, heart-made home.

A certified Culinary Nutrition Expert with TV training, Crystal teaches craft and cooking classes in her local community as well sharing craft and food ideas on TV. She is a lover of rainbow colors, sparkles, stickers, brightly colored sharpies, books, dark chocolate, tea, and of course her Cricut!

Crystal resides in British Columbia, Canada, with her husband, Rob; her daughter, Bella; son, Adam; and their two rescue dogs, Mochi and Marley.

Find more of Crystal and Hello Creative Family at:

Website: hellocreativefamily.com
Facebook: facebook.com/hellocreativefamily
Pinterest: pinterest.com/hellocreativef
Instagram: instagram.com/hellocreativefamily
By email: crystal@hellocreativefamily.com

Share your projects on Instagram by tagging **@hellocreativefamily** and **#hcfcricutcrafts**